AT HANKA'S TABLE

AT HANKA'S TABLE

BY

HANKA SAWKA

WITH

HANNA MARIA SAWKA

Lake Isle Press

Published by Lake Isle Press, Inc.
16 West 32nd St., Suite 10-B
New York, NY 10001
(212) 273-0796
E-mail: lakeisle@earthlink.net
http://www.lakeislepress.com

Distributed to the trade by:
National Book Network (NBN), Inc.
4501 Forbes Avenue, Suite 200
Lanham, MD 20706
1(800) 462-6420
http://www.nbnbooks.com

Library of Congress Control Number: 2004093908

ISBN: 1-891105-09-4

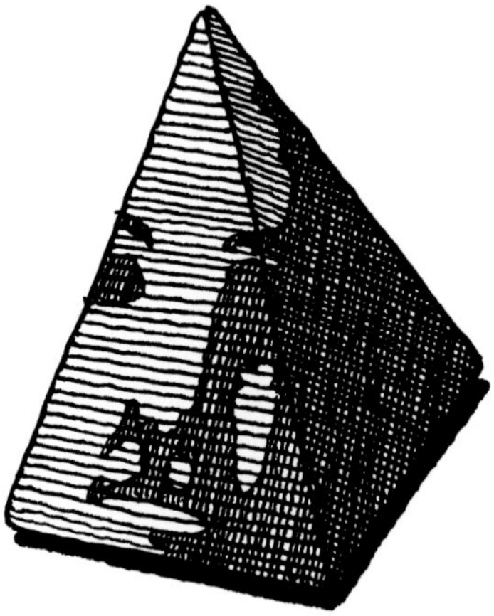

Cover and text art: Copyright © Jan Sawka
Book design: Janusz Kapusta
Photo credits: Susumu Sato, pages 128-129, photos 3, 4, 5;
Marcin Drękowski, page 163, photo 5

10 9 8 7 6 5 4 3 2 1

Printed in China

Dedicated to my mother, Krystyna Miłoch Maletz and my in-laws, Jan and Maria Sawka.

Acknowledgments

Great, great thanks to Hiroko Kiiffner,

for your belief in this project,

for making it happen

and for your warmth, wisdom,

and patience all the way through!

Thank you Shining Sung

for being the match-maker

behind this project!

Thank you Frank Boyer

so much for your friendship, support,

and help in finding ways to say things that

sometimes were so hard to explain!

Thank you Graciella Torres Brown

for your helping hands, energy, and smiles

during the photography sessions!

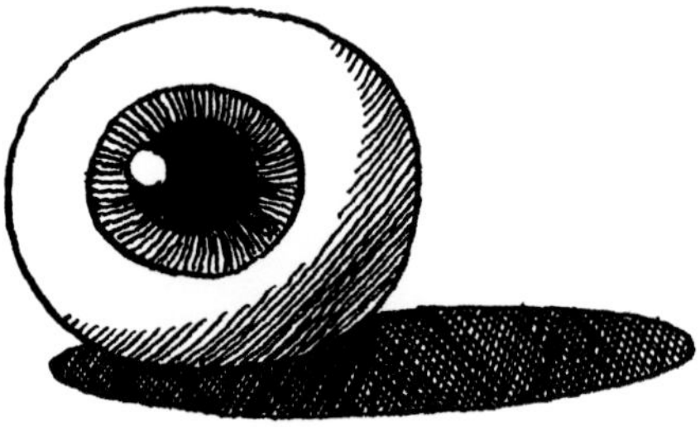

Contents

Introduction

As a child, I dreamed of an interesting life full of the colors, flavors, and vistas of new and distant places and cultures. Unfortunately, I was born in what was then communist-occupied Poland, a few months after Joseph Stalin died.

Poland belonged to the "lesser" Europe, cordoned off from the rest of the world by the Iron Curtain. Communism, touted by its government as the most humane ideological system, was in reality a regime that brought poverty, censorship, and never-ending shortages of food and other staple goods to its citizens. Daily life was blank and colorless, and precious time was spent finding the necessities for a normal life—a piece of fruit, a pair of shoes, a battery for the radio, or a pair of jeans.

While growing up, I learned about the real history of my country and the world from my mother and grandfathers, for the educational system tried to instill a "truth" fabricated in Moscow. Poland had been losing her wealth and power for the past few centuries, and worse yet, she had lost her independence completely during the nineteenth century. After a brief moment of freedom after the First World War, Poland was again invaded and enslaved, first by Nazi Germany, then immediately afterwards by the Soviet Union.

But the spirit was still there; people fought back with their wit and persistence to lead normal lives, to be Europeans as they had been for millennia. Poles fought to have their own culture and customs, the luxuries of friendship, good food, and healthy self-esteem.

Beginning when I was a teenager, I helped prepare for family and religious holidays and ceremonies. I learned how to cook quickly, economically, and with good taste. In this respect, my mother prepared me well for adult life. When I grew up, I met and married Jan Sawka, an accomplished painter, printmaker, and poster artist who also had strong interests in theater and music. As a young artist, Jan's life in communist Poland was extremely difficult. But then again, what young artist, in any country, leads an easy life?

I did my best to create a sense of luxury; a good meal for us, and the ever-present group of fellow artists, was always the high point of our simple life. It eased our miseries and created a small exile from everyday troubles. Then we left Poland in rather dramatic circumstances. We started a whole new life, first in France, then later in the United States. We were caught up in a seemingly endless process of rebuilding our lives and accommodating to new cultures and customs, often having to re-establish Jan's career almost from scratch. New households were created, new friends gathered around. I did my best to have them well fed, so that together we could forget about our daily troubles. My Polish cuisine underwent constant change: I added new spices and dishes that I saw around me in these new countries. Newcomers to our circle helped to enrich the menu as well.

All the while we fought hard to establish Jan's position in the art and design scene. At the same time we tried to create comfortable and warm conditions to raise our only child, Hanna. It was up to me to keep things going, from basic homemaking to entertaining for the many guests, partners, collaborators, art critics, dealers, and collectors ever present in our lives. Jan has always discussed all aspects of his work and professional problems with me; we decide together about the key moves. Our marriage is a true partnership with our roles closely intertwined; it takes two not only to tango but also to build success in the art world.

Nowadays, with the old battles behind us, we travel a lot, meet even more great people, and see new places. We soak up new cultures, and I enjoy learning culinary customs from all corners of the world. We come back home with new tastes, new recipes, and new ingredients to further enrich our table.

Times do change, but the challenges remain high. Jan's battlefields are not confined to the small island of Manhattan; we also go to work in Japan, Europe, and the Middle East, and we visit Poland, now free and struggling to rebuild herself. I suddenly see how great is the culinary tradition of my old homeland and enjoy tasting a true renaissance of Polish cuisine.

I would like to show young people starting their own lives that by cooking simply and imaginatively, one can help loved ones and oneself immensely in daily struggles, creating a true luxury. It is easier to dream about lofty projects around a great dinner with friends. My book describes the troubles, victories, and complications of a life that I would never have imagined as a young girl some thirty years ago. My childhood dream has been fulfilled. The price was very high, but who says that life is easy?

Chapter 1

Growing Up Under Communism

Before my life became an adventure of travels and meetings with people, I grew up in a country that was like a great big prison. Life there was so bleak and absurd that the young people in Poland today can hardly imagine it, let alone people in countries lucky enough to have a history of democracy and civil rights. To understand my entire story, however, I must first offer you this chapter, tainted with sad and difficult memories though it may be.

I was born into a family of physicians in the city of Częstochowa during the dark times of the communist occupation. I came to life as a twin; my identical sister's name is Ewa. Ewa and I have a sister two years older, Olga. Just a decade before we were born, the Nazi occupation had ended; millions of Poles had died at German hands. Like so many other Polish families, there were losses in our own family. Two of my great-uncles, both lawyers, died in Auschwitz. The wife of another of my great-uncles was shot in Ravensbruck, a death camp for women, for her role in establishing a resistance organization within the camp.

In 1945, Poland was "liberated" by the Russians. What in fact happened was that a new occupier took over the country. We Poles could not see this as liberation, for the Soviet army had invaded Poland in 1939, seventeen days after the Nazis. They had committed atrocities comparable to those of the Nazis, but the new communist government carefully covered this up.

I remember one day, when I was a little girl, I came home from school and found my grandfather Feliks crying. He was the rock of our family, and I had never seen him cry before—I was shocked. He was crying because he had just learned that a book had finally been published in the West by Polish émigrés about the Katyń Massacre, an atrocity perpetrated by the Soviet army under Stalin's orders. In 1939, 25,700 unarmed Polish army officers, prisoners of war captured during the Soviet invasion, were secretly executed. These men were a substantial part of the Polish educated class. This was how I learned about this crime for the first time, for mention of the word *Katyń* was forbidden in Poland, just as no one was ever supposed to know about the regime quietly killing "inconvenient" Poles during the late '40s and early '50s. To this day, secret torture and death chambers are still accidentally discovered beneath the streets of the capital, Warsaw, as well as in other cities.

Most Poles felt the impact of the new occupation in the denial of civil and human rights and in the poverty of their everyday lives. The new system had all sorts of convoluted ways of limiting people's freedom, of which the compulsory registration of all members of the population is a good example. Americans, who are free to move from place to place, may have difficulty imagining that a person had to register at one address in one city, and that was the only place where one could legally abide. To move one's place of residence from one city, or even street, to another, one needed a formal permit issued by the police under instructions from the Party. Getting this paperwork done was a slow process, resulting in confusing, anxiety-provoking situations. Every citizen over eighteen years old was required by law, on penalty of arrest, to carry his or her domestic passport, an identification booklet that indeed looked like a small passport. Besides giving a description of your person, the booklet stated precisely where you were registered and where you worked. If information was missing or had expired, the owner of the passport could be arrested as "an unproductive element of society."

Owning a home was an almost impossible dream for people. Families would save up for decades to purchase a cramped apartment. A committee oversaw the construction of new apartment buildings, blocks of concrete slabs with small cubicles, windowless kitchens, and microscopic "balconies" that were good for cats, but not for people. Young couples often had to wait for years before they could have a place to settle down together.

A car was another nearly impossible dream. A small car with a two-cylinder engine was worth five years of a doctor or engineer's salary. And almost every valuable product was subject to a rationing system. This meant items such as cars, apartments, color TV sets, and washing machines were available only to selected purchasers through Party channels, large factories, schools, or military bases, creating a huge black market that was at times almost bigger than the legal economy. Prices for such black market items were several times higher than on the open market. Besides all the inconveniences and humiliations this system generated for its citizens, you can imagine to what extent a burgeoning bureaucracy quickly developed, slowing down all affairs of the country and of the people.

As I've said, the country was like a giant prison; it was almost impossible to physically get out. Obtaining a passport and an exit visa was a true miracle for an ordinary citizen. If one somehow managed to be granted a visa, one faced yet another obstacle, namely, how to travel on the amount of money that a citizen was officially allowed to carry. Regardless of the length of your trip, you were limited to about one hundred dollars per person. And Polish currency, like the currencies of all the communist countries, was nonexchangeable.

The majority of citizens were rarely granted passports to visit the West, but they were permitted to visit Romania or Bulgaria or even the "communist paradise," the Soviet Union. Excursions to the Soviet Union were allowed only in organized groups that were first carefully screened by the secret police and accompanied by a small squad of Polish militia. Every person was considered a potential enemy, so, after crossing the border into "paradise," the group was guarded by additional Russian KGB agents. When I was seventeen, I visited Moscow with students from my class on an exchange and found that KGB officers even followed kids like us! I recall a tiny fifty-year-old KGB woman agent, who looked as if she might have walked out of a James Bond movie (of course, not as one of his girlfriends). People sometimes did manage to escape, crossing the sea to Sweden or finding other ways to the free world. When a son or daughter

escaped abroad, however, revenge on their family was incredibly swift and brutal; the parents were fired from work and siblings were thrown out of universities or from their jobs.

The people to whom the above description did not apply were the Red bourgeoisie. This class represented another paradox, or maybe it was a direct result of this sick system. Despite official dogma about equality and the workers' class governing the country, comparing Party members to the masses would be like comparing the Rockefellers to American farmers. They were completely unaccountable members of society. To quote George Orwell's *Animal Farm*, "some were more equal than others."

They lived in a different world: Their children were born in private Viennese clinics, or at least in the special military clinic near Warsaw (for lesser comrades). Young Reds attended the best Western universities, Moscow being reserved for the lowest party members' young. Later, when Jan and I settled in the West, we met many of them, the very children of our oppressors in Paris and New York, often posing as victims of the Red regime back home.

Health care and vacations (spas and recreational facilities created for the few) were off-limits to "the working class that would lead the country to its sunny future." The Reds established a whole system of "off-limits" stores. The lowest level of such stores served the militia (police) and the local representatives of the regime. Next, militia and army officers, higher-level Party members, and leaders of state-owned industry could shop at slightly better outlets. Aside from basic food staples, imported items were occasionally sold there at far cheaper prices than one would find in ordinary stores. Even our famous Polish ham was exported or available to the Red elite only. Higher up, in Party headquarters, there were classy boutiques open only to the elite, including diplomats from "brotherly countries," where Russian caviar and French brandy were sold.

Meanwhile, on a day-to-day basis, the communist system painfully denied ordinary people the most basic of goods. The lack of food and consumer goods was so appalling that it was surreal. Everything was centrally planned by ideologues with no understanding of realistic economic, market, or supply-and-demand dynamics. They were most often recruited on account of loyalty, not necessarily because they were the brightest members of society. The great hero of the Solidarity movement, Lech Walesa, once stated that if communism were established in the Sahara Desert, within two years sand would have to be imported from abroad.

Even something as unromantic as toilet paper rarely appeared in stores, despite the Party Central Committee's reports of "an increase in toilet paper production at the plant named after V.I. Lenin." I remember a photo published in an English newspaper in the 1980s showing a young, well-dressed woman walking down a Warsaw street with a huge necklace of a dozen toilet paper rolls on a string, a great trophy of her daily shopping.

The problems with food rations were so severe and constant that we were aware of them even as small children. Topics such as when something would be "thrown" to the stores and in what quantity (quality was never discussed; it was consistently poor) and how much it would cost were so persistent among adults that we got a picture of it very early in our lives. Oranges, figs, bananas, and pineapples were so scarce that most people never knew how they tasted. The only time food supplies were slightly better was before Christmas and, to a lesser extent, around Easter.

Culinary arts and the tradition of Polish dishes celebrated over the centuries were crucial in preserving the culture and spirit of an enslaved and impoverished nation. For a poor, oppressed people, entertainment and luxuries were rare. Restaurants were few and usually awful, as food was scarce and expensive. People stayed home to eat and entertain. Every hostess tried her best to produce a lavish and elegant party with elaborate dishes that showed her individualism and inspiration. Women spent many hours hunting for specialties, trying to buy "rare" foods: meats, vegetables, and fruit for such occasions.

For Christmas, Easter, New Year's, and family celebrations such as name days or wedding anniversaries, tables were full of good food, and vodka flowed in the cramped, crowded apartments across Poland. Every dinner party turned into a heated political discussion or a nostalgic evening in which grandparents recalled the glories of Poland's distant past, or even of the short twenty years of independence between the Great Wars. In this modest but meaningful way, people celebrated brief moments of happiness, intimacy, friendship, and independence. We lived in a country within a country, a double life of survival and remembrance.

My family was relatively privileged, both parents being physicians, but those privileges are quite laughable when compared with the life of an American doctor. My mother became single when we were little, and she had to struggle on her own to give her three daughters a decent childhood. Never in her life was she able to purchase the communal flat in which we grew up or to own a car.

My mother worked as a family doctor from early morning until suppertime at the local clinic. This was a state-run facility with very poor conditions and an equally appalling pharmaceutical supply; a few nurses and hordes of sick patients crowded the small waiting room. During influenza epidemics, my mother had to treat around sixty patients a day, including home visits, which she had to get to on foot or by bus.

My mother's salary in no way matched the amount of work she had to do. Although well educated, professionals were paid extremely low salaries to make the point that Poland was a country belonging to the working class and not to the middle class. Ironically, these workers weren't much better off, as they were literally worked to death in mines and polluted factories. Our mom was much liked by her patients. She also ran a little after-hours private practice out of our flat. It enabled her to barter her medical services for basic food, a decent winter coat, prime beef cuts, or rare oranges.

As we grew, my sisters and I started to understand the realities of life—the life of our family as well as that of Poland after the last war. As a child, I didn't understand the complications that history had created for my country, but I felt, as did all children of my age, that something very basic was wrong with almost everything in our lives.

My home town, Częstochowa, is a city famous for its majestic, Baroque-period Bright Mountain Monastery, whose crown jewel is an ancient portrait of the Black Madonna, an object of cult worship and a sacred symbol to millions of Poles. Our apartment faced the main street with its stores and a few restaurants. If not for the monastery, with its priceless collection of artworks, formidable fortifications, and an ornate church dominating the area, Częstochowa would be another drab, poor, industrial city in postwar Poland.

The Bright Mountain Monastery offset the communist slogans and propaganda that crowded every day of our lives. Posters bearing slogans lined the streets, claiming that the Party cared for every citizen, like a "mother of the nation." In my city, St. Mary, envisioned in the Black Madonna painting, was a source of spiritual comfort and hope to people, standing in bold contrast to the manufactured promises that were empty to people living hard and bitter lives.

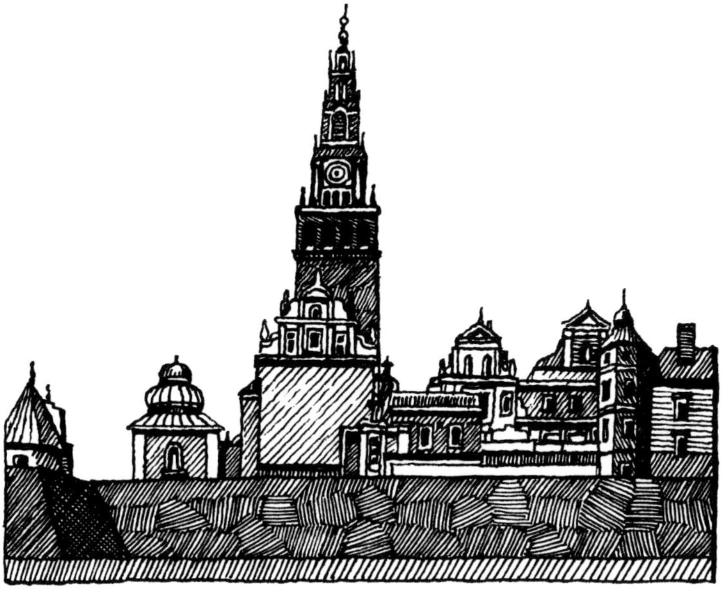

While I could visit the beautiful monastery up the street, directly under our apartment windows was also a place that represented the Party's "motherliness," a paltry meat shop owned by the nationalized food corporation. This was a system where incentives were nonexistent and people worked to further the communist ideal. A select few were allowed to be in business privately; these were the shoemakers, tailors, and other craftspeople, but for the most part, private ownership was banned by the system. Nationalized businesses, in general, functioned very inefficiently and inadequately, and our local butcher shop was an excellent example.

During the day, the butcher shop, a rather big space, was totally empty. The reason was easy to spot instantly: tired-looking pieces of meat on a few hooks and a dirty slab of lard were the only items to interest potential buyers. The shop was resupplied once a week or so, in the early hours of the morning. The shop opened at 7 AM, but already by 4 AM a crowd was queuing up, the line often stretching a block long. The moment the shop was opened, the wild crowd of people, mainly women, would attack the entrance, trying to get inside first. The supplies usually lasted for the first thirty to forty buyers. Some people were injured in such melées; living above the battle scene, my mother helped people many times. Sometimes, waiting for hours in cold weather, older or weaker clients-to-be would faint. Now picture these situations happening daily across the whole country and in fact across the whole world of Socialist Democracies, as the poor European countries under Soviet control were called.

According to the traditions of the Catholic Church, Friday is a meatless day. As Poland is predominantly Catholic, this tradition has been and is respected to this day. At one point, the regime introduced another meatless day, Meatless Monday, which was meant to further restrain people from consuming meat. A joke circulated among the people after Monday was declared meat-free: Mr. Gomułka, the First Secretary of the Polish Communist Party was asked to come to the Vatican. There he learned that the Pope had declared him a saint for his further contributions to Catholic discipline. Poles did their best to laugh these situations off, and at the same time, they were becoming more creative at making a healthy and varied vegetarian kitchen in the face of food shortages. Without a broad selection of ingredients to properly replace meat, one had to be resourceful, and it was a struggle just to meet nutritional requirements.

Chapter 2

The Past Storms of My Country and My Family

With all the trials communism afforded us, Poles had to depend on a strong national will to sustain their culture, religion, and sense of nationhood. Although Poland was separated from Europe by a wall of minefields and a repressive system, it never ceased to be a true European nation. Growing up and learning about complicated historical and political matters, I became aware that I must be independent and able to cope with almost anything that fate would deliver. On the other hand I was learning to be tolerant of everyone, regardless of race or faith, profession or persuasion. What helped me to understand this was the unusual history of my family. It was within families, after all, that the Polish spirit had been preserved.

My country's name means "land of fields." Poland is literally that, occupying a place on a broad plain, closed only in the north by the Baltic Sea and in the south by mountains. The fields have been wonderful for agriculture, while the open western and eastern borders encouraged trade—though they were less of an advantage when a neighbor was in a warlike mood. When Poland was powerful during the Renaissance, our neighbors weren't thrilled by the lack of natural borders either. For better or for worse, Poland is a country on a crossroads, and people of many nationalities have assimilated with the Poles. My family is a good example, my grandparents from both sides being of French, Russian, and German origins. God only knows who else is included in the genealogical tree.

My grandmothers died early, so it was only my grandfathers whom I knew well. My paternal grandfather, Jan Maletz, and his father and grandfather were musicians. They came to Częstochowa from Germany; my great-grandfather was hired to found the symphony orchestra of the Bright Mountain Monastery. A German married to a French woman, they traveled to places that offered opportunities for work; in their case it was Poland.

Grandfather Jan was trained as a pianist at the St. Petersburg Conservatory. He returned to Poland when the Bolshevik Revolution broke out. Despite his musical training, after the war he worked as the local postmaster. Thanks to his unceasing passion for music, my sisters and I were introduced to music at a very young age. We often accompanied him on walks around the Bright Mountain Monastery. He had grown up there, and his stories amazed us.

My maternal grandfather, Feliks Miłoch, was a doctor. During the Second World War he cared for wounded and sick soldiers from the many underground partisan groups fighting the Nazis. Later he carried on his work, treating civilians in surrounding villages. His wife, Maria, was a teacher and linguist, very popular in the whole area, thanks to her dedication to education regardless of the ideological system. When she and later my grandfather died, almost the entire city marched in their funeral processions. Such a large funeral gathering was an unusual and bold statement in communist Poland, where public assemblies were absolutely forbidden, unless state sponsored.

My grandfathers, Jan and Feliks, played a fundamental role in passing down the knowledge of our country's history and traditions. They taught us the real history of Poland and of the world and pointed out the nonsense of communist propaganda and policies. This was important, as our schools were teaching an ideologically doctored version of history. Basically, the authors of our textbooks made past history look awful, proving that communism just had to happen to save the world. However, it was hard for us to imagine things ever being much worse than what we knew!

Not only was our history being changed, the system was trying to change our language. Prewar Polish was declared to be bourgeois, with too many noble and Christian associations. A form of newspeak evolved, an extreme political correctness, where even such words as *underwear* and *lamp* were replaced. Underwear, depending on the sex of the wearer, was called masculine or feminine triangle. Communism also penetrated the realm of religion and tradition, creating substitutes for various ceremonies. For example, there were communist holidays with particular rituals and sermonlike speeches. A church wedding was not a legal marriage, rather, a civil "wedding," with its substitute "mass" was required. A church wedding could only be arranged after the civil marriage had taken place.

The Western world was presented as a place of moral and psychic decay rampant with prostitution, drugs, poverty, and crime. These terrible problems of the decadent West, they insisted, were "nonexistent" in Poland and the other communist countries.

Thus, we quickly realized that two truths existed in Poland: one that we learned at our highly controlled school, the other we learned at home. We never trusted the former, but we never said a word about the latter outside of home. Millions of young people in other occupied parts of Europe learned about the world in the same way.

We learned about the glorious days of the Piast and Jagiellonian dynasties, which defended Europe from Asian invaders. During the Renaissance, the Polish aristocracy, one of the oldest in Europe, built a huge and wealthy nation that extended from the Baltic to the Black Sea. Poland was one of the richest European kingdoms; her wheat and other agricultural products were selling well around the whole continent. Her strong rulers were leading European sovereigns, providing security and prosperity for their people. Science and the arts flourished, enriched by connections with Renaissance Italy. Copernicus, who revolutionized science by proving that the world revolved around the sun and not the other way around, was Polish. And Poland had the first democratic constitution on the European continent.

I also learned of the country's painful decline over several centuries. Long wars, the collapse of agriculture, and domestic unrest led Poland through a steady downward spiral. Finally, in the eighteenth century, the partitions started. The more powerful neighbors, Russia, Prussia, and the Austro-

Hungarian Empire annexed Poland part-by-part. By the end of the century, the once-powerful independent nation had ceased to exist. Poland disappeared from the political map of Europe and was plunged into a 123-year occupation. The most severe occupiers were the Russians and Prussians. Their repression of Polish culture included a ban on the use of Polish language in schools, liquidation of the universities, and restrictions of the economy and industrialization. Despite the harsh treatment of the occupying powers, Poles fought back, sometimes very violently.

Two major uprisings, in 1830 and in 1863, took place against the most brutal occupier, Russia, but the superior power of the Russian army crushed these rebellions, killing many young Poles; thousands were exiled to Siberia, and thousands fled the country. The Poles fought on, inspired by the memory of Tadeusz Kościuszko, a great patriot, who had led a failed insurrection against the Russians in the late eighteenth century. Prior to the uprising, Kościuszko had been an officer in the American Revolution, where he served as a strategist and military engineer. He later contributed to the writing of the United States Constitution. Upon his death, he designated the land and money earned for his wartime contributions to be used toward the freeing and educating of American slaves. A symbol of the fight for freedom, Kościuszko was in my thoughts as I made my way to America.

Among those exiled to Siberia during those dark days were the parents of a man who made his mark on world literature: Józef Konrad Nałęcz Korzeniowski, now known by his English name, Joseph Conrad. An example of the many gifted Poles forced into exile, Conrad left home around the same age as I did. I often think of him when I look back on my travels; perhaps that is one of the reasons he remains my favorite writer.

Death and exile were not the only punishments for the nineteenth-century uprisings. Many of the land-owning gentry, stripped of property, had no recourse but to migrate to the cities, where they eventually assimilated into the urban middle class. This urban-gentry mix was the beginning of what is known to this day as the Polish intelligentsia, those with limited means, but with the background and education of the upper and middle classes. These patriots continued to cultivate Polish culture and traditions despite the prohibitions of occupation. It was within this group that Polish cuisine evolved and matured, blending the experiences and tastes of the city and the countryside.

Despite its occupation and struggles, Poland's strong sense of history and spiritual integrity aided its independence in 1918, after the First World War. I learned from my grandfathers about how, after twenty short years of intensive rebuilding, Poland was again defeated, first by Nazi Germany and then later by the Soviet Union under the pretense of "liberation." Although I learned this history in secret, little did we know then that one day, thanks to the preservation of our national identity in the home and the church, we would live to win our freedom back!

Easter in Poland

For centuries, the Kingdom of Poland was host to numerous ethnic and religious groups, namely, Jews, Gypsies, Protestants, Eastern Orthodox Christians, and even some Muslims. They helped form a multi-cultural society, and provided diverse culinary influences. The partitions of Poland, World War II, and Stalinism put a brutal end to this society, with genocides and mass migrations that left Poland virtually homogeneous. Ninety-five percent of present day Poland is Roman Catholic.

Traditionally, Easter is the most important holiday of Catholicism, making it the main religious event in Poland. During the dark days of Poland's occupations, the holiday took on a national meaning as well, especially with the arrival of fascism and later communism, both atheistic systems. Going to church and religious observances in the home became in themselves a form of protest, a factor that may partially explain the church's strength in people's lives to this day.

The Easter meal includes some of the most traditional Polish recipes known. It also combines Slavic traditions that pre-date the arrival of Christianity to Poland, more than one thousand years ago. The celebration of Christ's rebirth comes during the spring, when nature is reborn, an important moment for pagan Slavs as well. Thus, the originally pagan tradition of painting eggs is a rich and varied craft to this day. Egg painting, or the making of *pisanki,* is so widespread and traditional that various regions have developed their own techniques and motifs over the centuries. The color red is a particular favorite to this day. Pagan Poles of long ago believed the color had magical qualities, especially concerning fertility. Many households, including mine, boil eggs along with the papery outer skins of onions, which we collect for weeks in advance. After simmering in the water and onion skins for around an hour, the eggs become a beautiful deep red-brown.

The Catholic religion requires the most rigorous fast of the year to take place before Easter—the Lenten fast, lasting six weeks, during which one should abstain from eating meat. In the past, when people took the fast much more seriously than they do today, Poles became very creative, making meals from vegetables and fish, especially herring, which is abundant in the Baltic Sea. People ate potatoes, cabbage, meatless white borscht, and kasha. It also meant abstaining from sweets and cakes, which is why, during the day before the fast begins (Fat Thursday), people eat their fill of *pączki* and kindling cookies.

After the fast, the Easter Sunday table has always been a veritable explosion of foods. Although there aren't requisite entrées, Easter tables are lavish and typically laden with roasts, hams, cold cuts, and jellied meats. The desserts, however, are mandatory, and you are sure to find *babkas* (a sweet yeast-based cake) and rich *mazureks* on the table. While the babka is tall and light, the mazurek is rather low and flat and very rich, filled with what were traditionally the most luxurious ingredients—dried exotic fruits, nuts, or citrus, which had to be imported from southern Europe. The mazurek dates so far back that its origins are uncertain, but people suspect that it comes from the Turks and their sweet and rich tradition of desserts.

A Polish Easter Table

Mushroom soup awaits guests at their place settings. Clockwise from front: Purple-Cabbage-Turned-Pink Salad; Duck Stuffed with Apples and Prunes; the basket of blessed contents; Carrots with Peas; Stuffed Eggs; Prune and Apple Sauce for Meats; and roast pork.

Babka

Makes one 10-inch cake

This is a traditional, sweet, yeast-based cake. Its name means "country woman." Babka is a wonderful addition to breakfast or afternoon tea. The keys to a great babka are energetic kneading and a draft-free kitchen. If the yeast gets chilly, it won't rise properly.

1 cup milk
2 teaspoons active dry yeast
1 cup plus 1 tablespoon sugar
3/4 cup raisins
6 egg yolks
2 teaspoons vanilla
1 tablespoon vodka or other hard liquor
1 teaspoon grated lemon or orange zest
Pinch of salt
4 1/2 cups all-purpose flour
1 cup (2 sticks) unsalted butter, melted, plus more butter for pan
Bread crumbs, for pan
1/2 beaten egg, for glaze
Hard Sugar Icing (page 33; optional)

Babka in the company of a lamb, which in one form or another must appear on an Easter table

1. Heat 1/4 cup of the milk to lukewarm. Pour it into a small bowl, and gently stir in the yeast and 1 tablespoon of sugar. Set aside until frothy, 10 to 15 minutes.
2. Cover the raisins with boiling water and let them sit for 30 seconds; strain, and set aside to cool.
3. Beat the yolks with the remaining 1 cup of sugar; add the vanilla, vodka, zest, and salt; beat until fluffy.
4. Heat the remaining 3/4 cup of milk to a boil. Place 1 cup of the flour in a large bowl, and add the boiling milk, combining thoroughly with a fork. Add the remaining 3 1/2 cups of flour and mix. Add the yeast mixture and mix well. Add the yolk mixture and start to knead. Add the melted butter. Knead energetically for 10 to 15 minutes.

Add the raisins and knead some more; the dough should be quite soft, yet not stick to your hands.

5. Form the dough into a ball and place it in a bowl. Cover the bowl with a clean dishcloth and set it aside in a warm place with no drafts until it has risen to twice its original size, about 1 1/2 hours.

6. Preheat the oven to 350°. Warm a 10-inch tube pan briefly in the oven while the oven heats. Grease the pan with butter and dust it with bread crumbs. Transfer the dough to the pan. Glaze the surface with the beaten egg. Set aside in a warm place to rise for 30 minutes.

7. Bake until light brown, 60 to 70 minutes. Remove and let cool for 10 minutes, then remove from pan. Do not serve until completely cool. If desired, coat with Hard Sugar Icing (page 33).

Gypsy Mazurek (Easter Cake)

Makes one 10-inch cake

1/2 cup raisins
5 eggs, separated
1 1/2 cups confectioners' sugar
1 tablespoon pure vanilla extract
2/3 cup all-purpose flour
1/2 cup finely chopped figs
1/2 cup finely chopped dates
1/2 cup finely chopped walnuts
2 teaspoons grated orange zest
1 ready-made 10-inch round wafer or homemade crust (recipe follows)

1. Preheat the oven to 350°. Cook the raisins in boiling water until tender, about 1 minute, then drain well. Set aside to cool.
2. In a large bowl, beat the egg whites with an electric mixer until soft peaks form.
3. In a separate bowl, use an electric mixer to beat the egg yolks with the sugar and vanilla until fluffy, about 3 minutes.
4. Gradually mix the flour into the yolk mixture. Add the raisins, figs, dates, walnuts, and orange zest to the yolk mixture. Mix well. Fold the egg whites into the yolk mixture.
5. Pour the batter onto the ready-made or homemade baked crust. Bake for 30 minutes.

Crust:

2 cups all-purpose flour, plus more for dusting
1/2 cup shortening
1/2 cup cold water
Pinch of salt
Unsalted butter, for pan
Bread crumbs, for pan

ɪypsy Mazurek
ʋith decoration
ɪspired by one
f Jan's paintings

1. Mix the flour, shortening, water, and salt together thoroughly. Form into a disk, wrap tightly in plastic, and refrigerate for 30 minutes.
2. Preheat the oven to 400°. Grease a 10-inch round cake pan with butter and dust it with bread crumbs.
3. On a lightly floured surface, roll out the dough to a 1/4-inch-thick10-inch circle; place it in the pan.
4. Bake until golden, about 20 minutes. Remove and set aside to cool.

Royal Mazurek

Makes one 10-inch cake

Crust:

1/2 cup (1 stick) unsalted butter, chilled
1 1/4 cups all-purpose flour
3 egg yolks
2/3 cup confectioners' sugar
1 teaspoon pure vanilla extract

Orange filling:

1 pound oranges, washed
2 lemons, washed
1 pound sugar
1 cup water
1/2 cup flaked almond

Hard Sugar Icing (recipe follows)

1. Make the crust: Cut the cold butter into the flour so as to form pea-size bits.
2. With an electric mixer, beat the egg yolks with the confectioners' sugar and vanilla.
3. Combine the flour mixture with the yolk mixture thoroughly.
4. Form the dough into a disk and refrigerate, wrapped in aluminum foil, for at least 30 minutes.
5. Meanwhile, make the filling: Chop up the whole oranges and lemons (skin included) and remove the seeds; discard the seeds. Put the oranges and lemons into a blender and liquefy.
6. Put the orange mixture, sugar, and water in a pot. Bring to a boil, stirring, then reduce and simmer, uncovered, for 1 1/2 to 2 hours or until the mixture thickens and clarifies, stirring occasionally. Remove from heat.

7. Preheat the oven to 400°. Roll the dough out into a 10-inch circle and place it in a 10-inch springform pan or tart pan. Bake until golden, about 20 minutes.

8. Spread the filling on the crust using a knife; dip the knife in hot water to avoid sticking. Sprinkle the almond flakes on top.

9. When the filling and crust are cool, decorate the mazurek by dipping a spoon into the Hard Sugar Icing and drizzling delicate lines of it on the surface. Do not overdo it, or the cake will be too sweet. Allow the icing to set before serving.

Hard Sugar Icing

This versatile icing can be used on Babka (page 28), gingerbread cookies, cakes, and other desserts.

2 cups confectioners' sugar, plus more as needed
Juice of 1 lemon
2–3 tablespoons water
1–2 teaspoons vanilla, rum extract, or lemon or orange extract

Place the sugar in a bowl. Add the lemon juice, water, and extract gradually to the sugar, mixing it with a fork into a thick paste; if it becomes too watery, add more sugar.

In addition to the babka and mazurek, an Easter table is not complete without the representation of a lamb, which symbolizes the sacrificial nature of Christ. In Poland, the lamb is shaped out of sugar (purchased at the bakery) or out of butter (usually made by the most capable sculptor in the family). Another mandatory item is the basket of blessed contents, containing colored eggs, salt and bread (traditionally used to greet guests in old Poland, as salt was a luxury), kielbasa, ham, babka, and whatever else the family thinks of. A few days before Easter, a member of the family will carry the basket to mass (usually children like to carry out this important duty), and after mass, the priest blesses all the baskets, sprinkling them with holy water. The baskets are often beautifully decorated, a sign of the imagination and talents within a family.

After the Lenten fast, after the preparations, and after attendance at the masses on Good Friday and Great Saturday, a family performs one more important tradition before dining: participants at the meal exchange eggs cut into quarters from the blessed basket with good wishes for the rest of the year. This warm moment brings everyone together, and it is in this atmosphere that the delicious meal begins.

The second day of the holiday, Easter Monday, takes on a very particular form in Poland—the Śmingus Dyngus (pronounced "shmeen-goose din-goose") tradition. This is a day when everyone, especially youngsters, throws buckets of water at one another and at the unsuspecting (well, nobody is particularly unsuspecting on Wet Monday) passerby. In the countryside, the most popular targets are the prettiest girls in the village, and packs of youths hunt them down with pails. In cities, Śmingus Dyngus brings out the imp in everyone as well, with some even pouring water out of apartment building windows! To tell the truth, it's almost impossible not to get wet, except by staying indoors all day. Even then, you are still likely to get wet, thanks to your loved ones, because the belief is that the dousing brings good luck. After all, no one who loves you would want you to miss out on some potential luck!

The origin of Wet Monday dates from the time of the christening of Poland in 966, when King Mieszko I took baptism and thus the entire nation, whom he represented, had to follow. The upper classes were baptized without any problem, but not everyone living in small villages, far away from the affairs of state, understood what was happening and why. Christening an entire nation was a great undertaking for which there was not always enough time for explanations and convincing. Thus, villagers were christened en masse, with water thrown at them!

Chapter 3

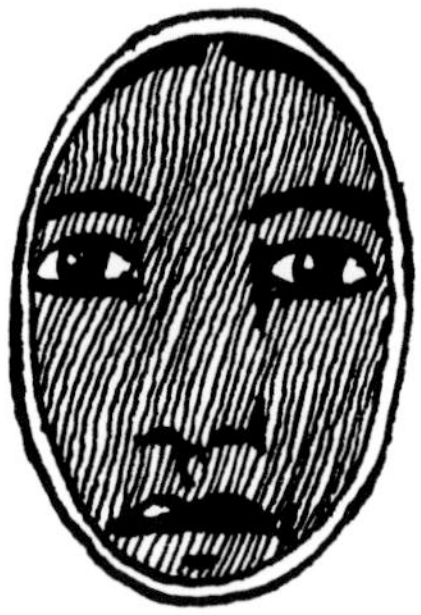

The Independent Polish Mother

Polish women had a very important role in helping the nation survive its dark times. The passing down of the culinary arts and domestic customs was a fundamental responsibility—a way to preserve Polish culture. It was important to celebrate, though in secrecy and on a small scale, the important religious and national holidays. Destiny gave this role to the women of Poland.

During the Polish uprisings of the eighteenth and nineteenth centuries and during the Great Wars, huge numbers of men were killed or exiled to remote Siberian wastelands. While some women accompanied their husbands in death or exile, many more remained at home to care for children, houses, land, and small businesses until their men, if they were lucky enough to be alive, returned. Women also had to perform all their usual duties, too. They ran farms and agricultural complexes, small mills and factories, while still educating their children, taking care of the elderly and sick, and of course, running their households. Their role in Polish history is legendary, and the figure of the Polish Mother has become a cultural icon. Pediatric and maternity hospitals are often named "Polish Mother," and statues of mother with child are popular in parks. The Polish Mother symbolizes strength and independence, and honors the role women played in saving the nation during its darkest hours.

My mother was forced to be very independent, but for a different reason. She divorced our father when I was about five years old. My father, a doctor, was very gifted and charming, but an irreversible womanizer. Although it was unfathomable to her neighbors, Mom threw him out of the house. From then on she paid dearly for this gesture of independence, unheard of in a provincial Polish city of the 1950's. As revenge, my father never paid any child support; my mother alone supported her three daughters. She nevertheless always found time to cultivate tradition in our household, in the spirit of women before her.

Lazy Noodles

Serves 2

The name comes from the fact that these noodles are so easy to make. They are usually a hit with even the most reluctant young eaters.

1 teaspoon salt
1 1/4 cups all-purpose flour
1 pound farmer's cheese or cream cheese
2 eggs
3 tablespoons unsalted butter, melted
Sugar and cinnamon, for sprinkling

1. Put a large pot of water with 1 teaspoon salt over high heat and bring to a boil; the noodles must be cooked immediately after being made.
2. Mix the flour, cheese, and eggs together thoroughly.
3. Roll the dough into a 1-inch-diameter cylinder. Cut the cylinder diagonally into 1/2-inch noodles.
4. Add the noodles to the boiling water immediately. Reduce the heat to medium and stir immediately to prevent the noodles from sticking to the bottom. Once the noodles float to the top, cook for 2 minutes, not more. Remove the noodles from the water with a slotted spoon.
5. Pour the melted butter over the noodles and sprinkle with sugar and cinnamon. Serve hot, as the noodles harden when cool. If they cool too quickly, due to a cold plate, for example, microwave them back to hot and tender.

My twin sister and I were born so small (me around three pounds, Ewa even less) that for about three months we had to be in incubators. If our mother had not been a physician we would have been a very short story. People would say that Mom gave us life twice. She had to keep an eye on us all the time, as far as our health was concerned. Ewa and I were very stressed, first by the failing marriage and then by the divorce. We were very poor eaters. Mom had to prepare healthy and light meals for us, fighting our tendency to not eat at all. Noodles were always a favorite dish.

Later, when we grew up, we saw our father sporadically and found that he had one positive point: his ardent rebellion against the political system. This was enough for us to gain some respect for him. When we would ask Mother about him, she defended him sometimes, explaining that his psyche was severely damaged during World War II. He was but fifteen years old when he joined the resistance. Perhaps that was reason enough, but then again she, too, had seen many wartime horrors herself.

Mother was a pretty teenager living in Częstochowa when the Nazis rolled in. Suddenly she was forced to learn Polish and Polish history in secret schools taught by nuns disguised as secular civilians. Polish clergy were also targeted by the Nazis. My grandfather, a doctor, would disappear at night to treat partisans in the forest. If caught, he, and maybe more of the family, would have been executed. This was happening right under the nose of an officer of the Wehrmacht, stationed in their home. Although the risk involved never stopped my grandfather, the family wondered if the officer really did not notice or if he were pretending not to see. One day he informed my great-grandmother that he was leaving, for he was being sent to the Eastern front. He went on to apologize to her for what his nation was doing, saying that he was deeply ashamed. He kissed her hand and told her that he would never return from the front. Indeed my family never heard from him again. He probably died in the terrible battle of Stalingrad.

My grandmother decided to send Mom to Warsaw where my great-aunt owned a pharmacy. The move was dictated by the fact that a locally stationed German officer had started to look at my mother with a sparkle in his eye. My grandmother decided that Warsaw would be a more secure place for her. Maybe as far as amorous German soldiers were concerned, but otherwise, how wrong she was!

Soon after her arrival in the capital, Mom had a close call with death. Nazis routinely rounded up people on the Polish streets. Some were selected to go to Germany for slave labor, others were sent to concentration camps to die (along with the three million Polish Jews killed during the war, another three million civilian Christian Poles were annihilated as well), and others were arbitrarily shot during the selection. These round-ups were one method for terrorizing the nation. One never knew when or where one could suddenly disappear or perish on the spot, and one could never be sure if loved ones would come home in the evening.

My mother was out with her cousin, the only son of my grandmother's sister, when German trucks blocked off both ends of the street and rounded everyone up into trucks. The helpless crowd was taken to the infamous Pawiak prison, where soldiers began selecting people for various awful destinations. Some were shot on the spot. My mother went through the horror of seeing her cousin suddenly taken aside and shot. She was crying when an anonymous German soldier approached her. He gestured for her to follow him, and he led her to the back of the building, where he let her free without a word.

Mom had been in Warsaw for but a year when the Warsaw Uprising broke out in August of 1944. This was the tragic attempt of independent Polish patriots to liberate Warsaw before the Red Army crossed the Vistula River. The two-month-long battle turned into a complete bloodbath for the Poles. Almost half a million fighters and civilians were killed. After this massacre, intending to break the nation's spirit completely, the Germans commenced the total destruction of the Polish capital. They blew up building after building. Literally eighty-five percent of the city was turned into rubble. Meanwhile, Stalin kept his superior army idling on the other side of the Vistula River. They calmly watched the destruction of the best Polish patriots and even shot those who tried to escape the inferno by crossing the river.

My mother came from a very patriotic family, so it was natural for her to get involved, despite her mere seventeen years. She worked as a field nurse for the uprising. It was a miracle that she survived. What she witnessed in this place of hell is material for another book. The crushing of the uprising ended all hopes of having an independent nation again, and Poland passed from one occupation to another. My mother was awarded a cross from the Home Army, the partisan army that the communists would later try to label a criminal organization; in fact this was the army loyal to the Polish government in exile in London.

After these experiences, Mom was convinced that formal education, supported by practical knowledge, were the best defenses against life's challenges, and that both were necessary in raising one's family. She said that the only wealth one really possesses is strength of mind and intellect. Coming from a Pole, it was easy to understand why such a point was made, because so many valuables—land, titles, rights, and property—were lost throughout Poland's stormy history. Mother repeated often that nobody can steal your knowledge and your education—short of killing you.

Despite the fact that she worked from early morning into the evening, mother kept total control over family life. With a firm hand she trained all three of us to learn as much as possible, at school and at home. To keep us out of trouble, mother filled our after-school time completely. We took piano lessons and dance classes as well as French and English lessons. At home, we participated in all domestic chores. Though only fourteen, I was able to prepare simple dishes and take care of the entire house. Mother, always busy at the public clinic, often gave us recipe instructions by phone.

Years later, in the United States, I raised my own daughter in this spirit, teaching Hanna the basics of day-to-day management. Beginning when she was twelve years old, I taught her to cook and bake. After we moved up to the country, and we had a bigger kitchen, Hanna was always helping me, especially for the holidays.

1. Mother and father's civil wedding.
2. Three sisters at the Baltic shore: to the left and right of Olga are Ewa and me.
3. Ewa and I, age 18, in Częstochowa.
4. My mother with a patient, a concentration camp survivor.
5. My mother with Ewa and me (upper left) at age four and dressed in traditional "Cracow" style costumes.

1

2

3

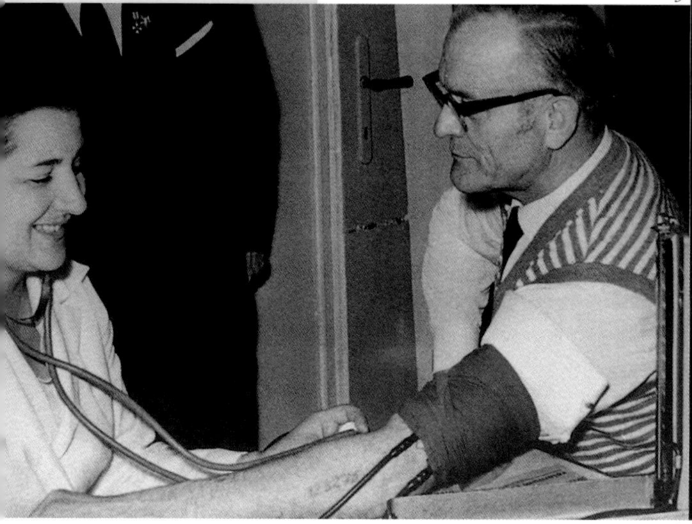

4

5

Chapter 4

The Beatles Behind the Iron Curtain

I grew up on the Beatles and the Rolling Stones' music. Despite the fact that the Iron Curtain separated us from the rest of the world, a surprising amount of free world culture, high as well as popular, reached us, particularly after the 1956 political thaw that followed Stalin's death. My twin, Ewa, and I frequented music concerts of all sorts. Movies and theater were our biggest passions. We devoured books, reading all the available classics and the increasingly popular American modern writers such as Hemingway, Faulkner, and Steinbeck, plus the emerging masters of South American literature, Cortazar and Marquez.

Częstochowa had only one repertory theater, with rather mediocre productions, but every Monday night national television aired the best productions with top actors from the Warsaw stages. After I moved (on account of my studies) to Warsaw, I went to the theater as often as possible. I was able to enjoy Polish masterpieces, and an array of Western playwrights, including Shakespeare, Molière, Ionesco, Beckett, Durrenmatt, Miller, O'Neill, Ibsen, Strindberg, and Pinter, among others. These moments were true paradise for us.

Despite the lamentable state of the economy, food shortages, appalling living conditions, and a regime totally controlled by Moscow, we had relatively easy access to the best artistic achievements from other countries. We couldn't buy a pack of Marlboros at the local store, but a ticket for a top production of a Samuel Beckett play cost only twenty cents.

We listened to rock music primarily on Radio Luxembourg, a fantastic station whose signal we received clearly without the interruptions characteristic of stations like Free Europe or the Voice of America. Powerful jamming devices on the western border of Poland silenced stations deemed as "enemy propaganda."

Western literature that made it past the censor's bureau (many books didn't) was translated into Polish and published in small numbers, market forces never mattering to central, or ideological, planners. Just borrowing a book for a weekend of intense reading was a true victory. The Central Bureau of Publications and Events, known as Cenzura (the censor's bureau), was ever present in our lives. In order to print a business card or an obituary, one had to apply to the censor's bureau. One never knew if the permit would be issued, or if it were rejected, why this had happened.

The censor's bureau had one positive point, however unintentional. We were free of tabloid magazines, trivial books about Hollywood wives,

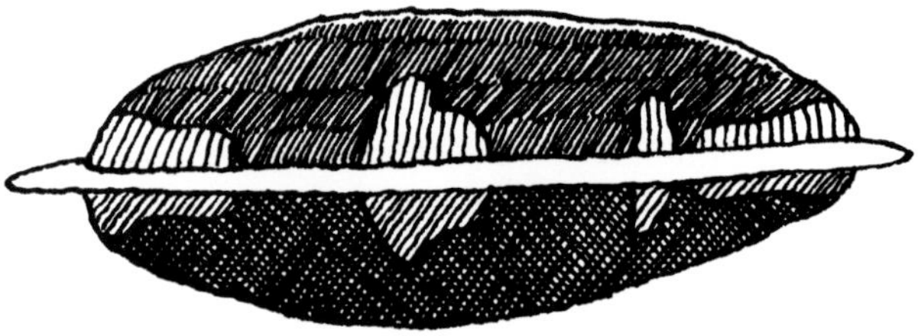

pornography, and comics. The same applied to the movies. Yes, naive and horrible communist propaganda films flooded our screens, but they were a minority, limited by small budgets and production facilities. The great artistic films of Kurosawa, Buñuel, Fellini, de Sica, Bergman, and Antonioni, as well as those of John Houston and John Ford, were shown frequently. On the other hand, Orson Welles' great masterpiece, *Citizen Kane,* was banned as a dangerous story of political corruption and tyranny.

When I was grown-up enough, another kind of literature started to sneak into my hands: the outstanding publications of *Paryska Kultura* (*Parisian Culture*), the Paris-based émigré publishing house specializing in authors and topics totally banned in Poland. To be caught at the border smuggling in such publications was a serious criminal affair and could mean the loss of a job or a career derailed. But it was, of course, a point of honor to read such literature; yet another form of defiance against the system.

In the late 1960s, an amazing musician shook up the stale prison our country had become. This was Czesław Niemen, who appeared on the scene very colorfully dressed, with what was then shocking and unprecedented long hair, an incredible voice, and songs full of meaning. Niemen was a rock star who was key in creating the counter-culture of Poland. His message was not about free love, but about freedom, and he did not sing about drugs or decadence; instead, the lyrics of his songs were the poems of banned Polish poets. Among them was Cyprian Kamil Norwid, a nineteenth-century Romantic poet who died young and who articulated the dreams of a then nonexistent Poland. Above all, though, what Niemen symbolized to the youth of Poland was a free man. He developed a huge following overnight—he caught on so quickly that the government couldn't stop him. The Central Committee met to discuss the outlawing of long hair for men, but they quickly realized that too many young Polish men were already sporting long locks, so no action was taken. It was also thanks to Niemen, in a way, that my future husband appeared in my life for the first time. One day, my older sister came home with a big and beautiful poster of the rock and roll idol. She proudly hung it up over her bed. This poster was by Jan Sawka, the man I would some day marry, and whom I would meet in a few months! It is moving to me that now, years later, Jan is using Niemen's music and compositions in his multi-media spectacle *The Voyage.*

Becoming a teenager, I started to care about my appearance. Naturally, like everything in Poland, the supply, quality, and trendiness of clothes were on par with the food and automobile standards, which meant poor design, poor workmanship, and a short supply. Finding a decent pair of pants or a winter parka bordered on a miracle. Shoes produced at centrally planned factories by untrained people were so uncomfortable and shoddy that everybody saved up money to order a wearable pair from a shoemaker. In terms of fashion, it was only on rare occasions that the Party would release some mildly stylish lines of clothing, but these were produced in such a great quantity that they quickly lost their appeal.

Again, as with food, Polish women were tremendously creative. I remember the remarks of John Darnton, the *New York Times* correspondent in Poland in the late '70s and early '80s. He stated that Polish women dressed so fashionably and colorfully that they looked like beautiful butterflies, contrasting sharply with the gray, dirty, and unrepaired streets of Polish cities. Young women were wildly ambitious, trying to look like the ladies crowding the Via Margutta, the Copacabana, or Carnaby Street, not to mention the Champs Elysées. To dress well, according to the latest Western fashions, was another form of protest against the dehumanization of individual life.

Like so many others, I never wanted to dress identically to one hundred thousand other Polish teenage girls, no way. My sisters and I made heroic attempts to find copies of French or German fashion magazines like *Elle* and *Burda*. Such magazines were sent by relatives living abroad (and often lost at customs offices; obviously there were enthusiasts of good fashion among the officers there as well) or smuggled in by the few lucky travelers.

When we managed to secure an issue of *Elle* for a day or two, we scrutinized its entire contents, noting which fashions could be mimicked or borrowed. Sometimes patterns were attached to the issue—what a lucky moment this was! We joined the hordes of young girls who were mastering their sewing skills or begging mothers or grandmothers to make a well-tailored creation. We did everything to shine at the one or two occasions during the Winter Carnival, when parties took place between the New Year and the Great Lenten Fast. There we enjoyed a moment of female triumph, flirting with the boys who had struggled to get a pair of real Levi's, and after the Beatles arrived, a pair of fancy boots.

After completing high school, I encountered another inequality of life in communist Poland. Favoring students from the working class, the regime established a special system of adding points to their university entrance exam results. Sometimes as much as fifty percent was added to their total scores, regardless of their achievements. Students not fitting the Party ideal—nobility, ex-landowners, families of prewar military and political figures, and people from the middle class—were thus made to compete against padded scores, and only outstanding candidates gained entrance.

My family dreamed of seeing at least one of us continue the tradition of working in the medical profession, so I tried my luck and applied for the entrance exams at the Warsaw Medical Academy. I passed all the exams, but scored a single point below the needed total score. Instead of being accepted to the medical department, I only qualified to study pharmacy. But there was a loophole, probably created by the frustrated physicians of Poland: after a year of pharmacy studies a student who marginally failed the test for regular medical studies was able to switch departments. With such a plan in mind I started to attend classes in the pharmaceutical department. Unfortunately, I hated the whole experience (Chemistry was my weak point) and soon elected to study psychology, which interested me more. Little did I know that soon there would be other changes in my life.

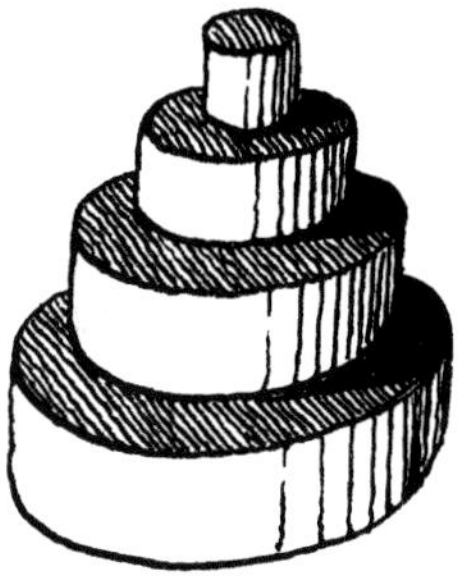

Chapter 5

Falling in Love

When I met my future husband, in 1973, he had long hair, round glasses, and jeans upon which he had painted colorful flowers. His dress code, which Niemen had brought into fashion, immediately announced that he was from the highly developed counter-culture. Individualism and the expression of the opposition was flowering in student theaters, illegally published books of underground poetry (known as *samizdats*—Jan illustrated some of the most influential ones), literature, and cabarets. Where one theater piece was taken down by the government, another would appear somewhere else; where a samizdat was being destroyed, another was being prepared. The regime really had its hands full as the opposition grew.

Things weren't always like this, though; before 1956 the Stalinist grip on Poland was very strong. Even jazz music was blacklisted. My father was a gifted musician, and while attending medical school, he played drums with the first jazz ensemble in Poznań, formed by the later famous pianist Krzysztof Komeda, who would go on to score Roman Polanski's film *Rosemary's Baby*. Their concerts were held in cellars; one could be expelled from university for such "antisocial" activities.

After 1956, censorship and cultural repression were loosened and the arts began to flourish. Polish graphic design, theater, film and literature were lauded internationally. The banal fact that Poles didn't have many options into which they could channel their energies was a contributing factor. No

matter how hard you worked at your job, you wouldn't get promoted if you didn't join the Party. If you came up with a way to earn more money, what would you spend it on anyway? If you put your energy into something creative, however, all kinds of magic could happen.

Culture was also used as a propaganda tool directed at the rest of the world. Poland hosted some of the most important events in the art world—poster and art biennials, and festivals celebrating film, music, and theater. Visiting these events was important to a Western artist's career so, ironically, Poles were able to have direct contact with some of the best international artists of the '60s and '70s. Polish artists also went to events in the West, though their visits were highly controlled. Mediocre artists clung to the Party, making more of a name for themselves at home. On the other hand, the system knew that quality was universally recognized, so they had no choice but to export good work. There was a fine balance between the system's need to exploit and control art, and the artist's need for free self-expression. This enabled someone like Jan to walk a tightrope—not giving in to the Party, but being able to go abroad, thanks to his talent. It was a difficult, but sometimes advantageous situation. When I met Jan, he had already visited many festivals in England, France, and other countries.

This tense relationship between the government and the arts was a tradition of sorts in Poland. During the Romantic period (c. 1822–1883), Poland's arts and culture were key in preserving the national identity, its political body having been partitioned off by its neighbors. Polish poetry and drama underwent a golden age; Fryderyk Chopin wrote his moving and patriotic music. Chopin's music and the poetry of such men as Adam Mickiewicz, Juliusz Słowacki, and Norwid contained hidden messages to their captive nation. My future husband and other artists of his generation continued, and were inspired by, this noble tradition of creating subtle works, with messages to be read between the lines. They learned to protest and to give hope and inspiration to their fellow Poles, in the face of tight control and censorship.

The meeting that would change my life forever happened while my two sisters and I were students in Warsaw. The oldest, Olga, was studying law (she and her daughter are now very successful lawyers in Warsaw), while

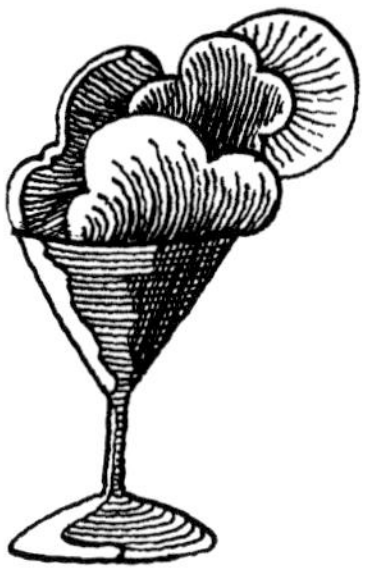

Ewa and I were studying psychology. Our mother had rented a flat for the three of us, and we were managing well, cooking our meals together.

One day my twin, Ewa, met two young artists at a party. She started dating one of them, Jerzy Czerniawski, an outstanding artist and poster designer. Soon after, Ewa invited me to their studio and I was introduced to him and to his flat-mate, Jan Sawka, because they hadn't believed that Ewa had an identical twin. I never would have expected that evening, in that small downtown apartment, to change my life. In fact, I was a bit annoyed, because the two men were speechless with amazement for a while, which didn't make for entertaining conversation! Soon after regaining his ability to speak, Jan invited me out for ice cream at Hortex, the best sweet shop in town. We talked for hours. The next day we met again and spent several hours discussing everything from recent films, books, and family affairs to politics, a particularly hot topic in our censored world.

The third time we met, Jan proposed to me. He declared that we were born for each other and nothing should part us. I was stunned. I was only twenty and I was not planning to marry anybody at such a young age. On the other hand, Jan was such a nice man and I didn't want to say no. I told him that we should just start dating and see what happens. Two weeks later, I made up my mind and said that I would marry him. I was in love and, despite reservations and my mother's warnings, I found myself starting a serious relationship. Ewa broke it off with Jerzy after a month, but I, an accidental visitor to the studio, was quickly "drowning" into this affair, maybe for life.

In his stubborn pursuit of me, Jan decided to introduce me to his family as soon as possible, so I met Jan's father and sister about two weeks after we started to date. Christmas was coming soon, and I was to spend the holidays at my mother's home in Częstochowa, so Jan arranged for me to join him in the mountains, at Krościenko in the Pieniny range, just after Christmas Day. A minor problem was Jan's dog, a huge German shepherd named Ares, who regarded Jan's rare visits home as a time to spend exclusively with him. Jan had had the stupid idea of coming home twice with previous girlfriends for brief visits, and both times Ares had behaved terribly toward the poor, scared ladies. He growled all the time and attempted to bite them, no kidding.

I was unaware of all this, and poor Jan nervously awaited me at the town's bus stop with nobody but Ares. My bus stopped, and when I saw Jan, I immediately jumped out of the vehicle, and into his arms. Halfway there, a huge dark beast leaped into the air. Jan was horrified, but quickly amazed to see that Ares was enthusiastically licking my face. We were best friends immediately.

With Jan's father, it was love at first sight. He was a cheerful man with a fantastic sense of humor. I must admit that I felt relieved by such a welcome. Jan was twenty-seven years old, a huge difference in age for me, a twenty-year-old "chick." Jan had already completed two master's degrees, in architectural engineering and in fine arts.

Jan Sr.'s family came from Galicia, the southern region of Poland. They were mostly Polish Catholics, though some were Eastern Orthodox Christians from Lemno, once a small Slavic nation in what is now southeastern Poland. Unlike his father, who worked in the Austro-Hungarian rail system, Jan Sr. was an architect and a caricaturist. Before World War II, he had belonged to the leftist bohemia of Lvov and Cracow. He was by no means a communist. Very few Poles were interested in communism, in fact, anything Russian was immediately suspect. Jan Sr.'s wife, Maria, also came from the Polish intelligentsia, her family being a mix of land-owning gentry and academicians from Cracow, some of whom worked at the famous Jagiellonian University. Maria had linguistic talent and a passion for teaching. She graduated from a high school specializing in teacher training and completed her studies at Jagiellonian University, where she majored in linguistics. Just before the war, she got a job at a large new progressive school near Tarnow, where she was to teach languages. She never got to her first day of classes. The first day of school that year, September 1, 1939, was the day the Nazi army invaded Poland, and the Second World War began.

During World War II, despite his deeply rooted pacifism, Jan's father did what so many Poles chose to do: after fighting a futile battle during the Nazi invasion of Poland, he escaped from his defeated nation to join other Poles who fought wherever and however they could. Some served as fighter pilots during the Battle of Britain; others sailed with the Atlantic convoys. Many, including Jan's father, joined the Allied armies as a military engineer. Meanwhile, Maria raised their daughter Anna alone, after taking refuge in their country house in Bochnia, near Cracow. Although he was fighting alongside the Nazis' enemies, Jan Sr. and Maria managed to communicate. They sent hundreds of coded letters and postcards past the Nazi censors in occupied Poland. Their "codes" were based on themes, characters, and places in literature and poetry.

In November 1945, Jan Sr. rejoined his wife and child in Poland. Upon his return, he was well equipped to contribute to the rebuilding of his devastated country. He had completed his architectural studies first in Lvov, and then in Switzerland, at the famous Winterthur Institute of Architecture, where one of his professors was Le Corbusier, a giant of modern architecture. Politically speaking, deeply disillusioned by Polish prewar right-wing politics, Jan Sr. strongly believed that socialism and a true democracy were the best hope for Poland's future. He disliked communism, but hoped that the new regime, established by Moscow, would accommodate a wide range of progressive people into their ranks, in order to pull the country out of postwar disaster.

His dream was short-lived, for first the Reds relocated the family from their beloved hometown, Cracow, to Hindenburg, a city newly recovered from Germany in Upper Silesia—a coal-mining region historically split between Poland and Germany. The city was renamed Zabrze. My future husband was born there in December of 1946. Soon after, Jan Sr. was arrested as a dangerous element, an "economic enemy," who had been trying to undermine the new order in Poland—an absurd accusation. Maria continued to raise her children alone. She was unable to find a job as a teacher from then on, and the reason was simple. As the wife of an enemy of communism, she could not be trusted to educate new generations. In the first years after the war, her language skills helped

her to survive, as Polish-Russian-German translating was in demand. As her skills became less needed, she turned to tutoring and finally, was reduced to knitting for a living. Jan and Maria were not alone in their situation. About a million Poles, mainly professionals and intellectuals, were arrested; some were executed, while the rest remained jailed without charges or sentences. I am all too aware of this during family gatherings that number just a handful now, cousins included.

Following Stalin's death in 1953, the regime started to reassess its inhuman policies, and began to release many of its prisoners starting in 1955. Jan's father was "rehabilitated," the term used for a former political prisoner, who has been reintegrated into society. Even though he was no longer in prison, his life, in effect, was permanently destroyed. He was forever listed as an enemy of the state in secret police files. This stigma was further extended to his son, my future husband, and thirty years later, to our daughter, Hanna. Jan Sr. regained his right to practice architecture, but despite immense talent and training, he worked at the lowest level of his craft. An "inconvenient" man politically, he was regularly fired or transferred from office to office.

Maria died less than a year before I met her son. A pity, as it was she who prayed to the Almighty to find Jan a wife such as me. Though we laugh when this topic is mentioned, Jan insists that it is true. When we returned to Warsaw after I met Jan's family, I moved into Jerzy and Jan's apartment. Naturally my Mom didn't know about it for almost nine months. When she visited the rented flat in which I was supposed to be living with my two sisters, I would hastily return and pretend that nothing was happening. My sisters never betrayed me. We knew how badly Mother would have taken it, for she always told us, "A girl from a good home never lives with a man before they tie the knot."

In the studio apartment, Jan and I shared the only bedroom, while Jerzy slept on a couch in the living room that also served as the studio. That is how I started to cook for everybody. The flat was furnished with the bare essentials, with chairs fashioned out of beer crates. The kitchen had almost nothing for cooking, but the whole establishment was squeaky clean. The budget was very small.

Jan was a fully trained artist, designer, and architect, but in communist Poland, a market for purchasing art was almost nonexistent. Only sporadically did the government's Ministry of Culture purchase the works of living artists, and what they paid was quite small. Private collectors were rare. Who could afford a painting, even a cheap one? The Red bourgeoisie were rich but never collected art; they were interested in other aspects of life—Mercedes cars and Russian mink coats for their mistresses.

Understandably, Mother was not amused by my sudden affair with Jan. She insisted that I first complete my studies, and then maybe the proper moment to tie the knot would come. The fact that Jan was an artist worried her. The stereotype of artists being hard drinkers, womanizers, and people rarely capable of earning enough money was powerful in her thinking. I tried to convince her that Jan was a new star in Polish art, internationally recognized for his posters, which at that time, were considered to be as important as Polish film and theater. Indeed, Jan was as respected in the visual arts as Roman Polanski in film and Tadeusz Kantor in theater. I argued that we would have a great future together. Mom was steady in her refusal. We tried to convince her, and during our visit to Częstochowa, in Jan's last attempt to ask for my hand, Mom used an old Polish traditional custom to say no. She served Black Soup—a very delicious dish based on duck's blood that is presented on the occasion of an unwelcome marriage proposal. Without a word uttered by the parents, the suitor learns how futile his attempt is when this plate of dark soup appears before him. Traditionally, the suitor must immediately leave the house of the young lady.

We sat down at the table, and I could not believe it when Mother produced Black Soup. We did our best to stay composed (I kicked Jan underneath the table to remind him to remain so) and...ate it. I finally broke the long silence, informing Mom that we were planning marriage regardless. She was silent and tense; Jan was equally uneasy. We quickly left her home to catch a night train to Warsaw. A week later she accepted our plans, reluctantly, of course. Now, after many years, I fully understand her situation; from her point of view it was a desperate attempt to save her daughter from almost certain disaster. I also remember my resolve, however, to press on regardless.

Black Soup

Serves 6 (including one rejected suitor)

This is an old Polish delicacy, traditionally served by a girl's parents to unwanted suitors as a "no." As for the blood, if you are not up to killing ducks (I know I'm not!), a butcher in a Polish neighborhood should be able to provide it.

1 onion
Blood from 1 duck
1 tablespoon vinegar
Parts from 1 duck: 2 wings, stomach, heart, liver, and neck
1 teaspoon salt, plus more to taste
6 cups water
1 parsnip, peeled
2 carrots, peeled
2 celery ribs
2 bay leaves
2 oz. dried plums
2 oz. dried apples
1/4 teaspoon freshly ground pepper
1/4 cup lemon juice
1 teaspoon sugar
Tiny noodles such as mini bowties, rice-grain pasta, or alphabets, cooked according to package directions and drained

1. Peel the onion and heat it on an open flame until browned on all sides.
2. Pour the duck blood into a bowl and immediately add vinegar. Set aside.
3. Put the wings, stomach, heart, liver, neck, 1 teaspoon salt, and 6 cups water into a large pot. Bring to a boil. Add the parsnip, carrots, celery stems, roasted onion, and bay leaves to the boiling mixture. Reduce the heat to low and simmer, covered, until the ingredients soften, about 2 hours.
4. Meanwhile, cover the dried fruit with hot water and soak for 1 hour.
5. Remove the fruit from the water and add to the simmering stock. Simmer together for at least 30 minutes.
6. Remove the stock from the heat and remove the meat, vegetables, bay leaves, and fruit. Reserve the meat and fruit.

7. Put the stock on medium heat and bring to a simmer. Slowly add the blood, stirring continuously. Add the lemon juice, sugar, and salt to taste.
8. Dice the reserved meat and fruit and add to the soup.
9. Divide the noodles among 6 bowls, add the soup, and serve.

My mother's reservations were not baseless, unfortunately. Jan was a brilliant artist, but his political problems were growing rapidly. His problems began with the Spring 1968 riots, while he was a student at Wrocław Polytechnic. In 1967, the Soviet Union announced an anti-Zionist policy, in reaction to Israel's occupation of the West Bank and Sinai. At the same time, parts of Eastern Europe saw a movement towards liberalization. Using its anti-Zionist campaign as a pretext, the Soviets began a purge of "dangerous elements" from Polish academia, culture, and politics. Subsequently, individuals defending those that were ousted were, in turn, deemed "dangerous." Students, including Jan, began to protest this crackdown on academic life. A leader in one of these riots, he was forced into hiding for six months afterwards. At the end of the year a partial amnesty was granted. Not a complete amnesty by any means, protesters had to spend three months in a special army battalion, at a camp "of elevated rigor," where they were "prepared" for five years of military service. The regime's goal was to punish and break them. While many of them, including Jan, were declared unsuitable for further military service after only two months, the greatest punishment was the permanent denial of many civil rights. Many were blacklisted and their careers destroyed, and some, their health and spirits broken, did not live long after their time in the punishment battalion.

I met Jan as he was moving to the forefront of the established arts—a field tightly controlled by the regime. His rising fame provoked restrictions, interrogations by the political police, frequent blacklisting, and long periods, sometimes six months, where Jan was unable to get commissions. When mom learned about this, she began to regard Jan with a warmer eye. Jan Sr. also won my mother over. When she met Jan's father and found that his upbringing and views were compatible with her own, mom finally accepted my man as her future son-in-law.

This was how I started my adult life with Jan. The first step I took was to buy dishes and silverware in order to serve my simple food in a civilized way. I was lucky, for a new store had opened just a week earlier in Warsaw that specialized in housewares. Before the supplies dried up, I purchased several sets of dishes and steel flatware. We carried our booty to the apartment triumphantly. What a day; everything was bought in one day without having to stand in a line extending for three blocks.

1 2

3 4

1. Jan's parents, Maria and Jan Sawka, in the mountain resort of Krynica, just before WWII.
2. Jan and I two months into our relationship.
3. Jan and I with 2-month-old Hanna in our Warsaw apartment.
4. Jan and I just after our civil wedding in Warsaw. I am wearing a dress Jan painted and we are standing beneath a monument of Jan Kiliński, a hero of the 17th century Polish-Swedish wars.

Chapter 6

The First Year of Marriage

As a freelance artist, Jan was forced to receive special certification from the Ministry of Culture confirming his legal status as an artist who works at home. His situation was further complicated by the fact that after the 1968 student riots he was permanently forbidden to hold a steady job—a huge problem, as Jan was basically forbidden to earn money. He was excluded from military service for life—the one part of his punishment that Jan cherished. The last thing he wanted to do was defend the "socialist paradise."

One of the most troublesome of Jan's restrictions was that he lost the right to live in communal apartments—the only type of housing available. This posed a significant problem with his citizen registration. Having no legal residence, he was constantly under the threat of arrest. Whenever a militia patrol would stop to check his documents, only the Ministry of Culture could prevent his arrest, and they had a vested interest in doing so. While living illegally in Cracow, Jan was a leading member of the alternative oppositionist theater called STU (the name was intended to suggest meaning, but had none). Because it wanted to create an illusion of free expression, the regime often chose STU to represent Poland at foreign festivals. The situation was convenient for the government; it used Jan, knowing they could expel him from Cracow at any time if he misbehaved.

Ironically, Jan, a walking political liability, was a big financial and propaganda asset for the regime. Jan himself earned a tiny sum for his work. For a complete original poster design (painted on a 40-by-30-inch board), Jan was paid the equivalent of sixteen U.S. dollars. Automatically, Polish authorities took ownership of all rights to a poster; no claims were possible by the artist. All earnings went to the government. Imagine our frustration when we visited galleries and boutiques in Paris or New York after we left Poland and saw his numerous posters with impressive prices.

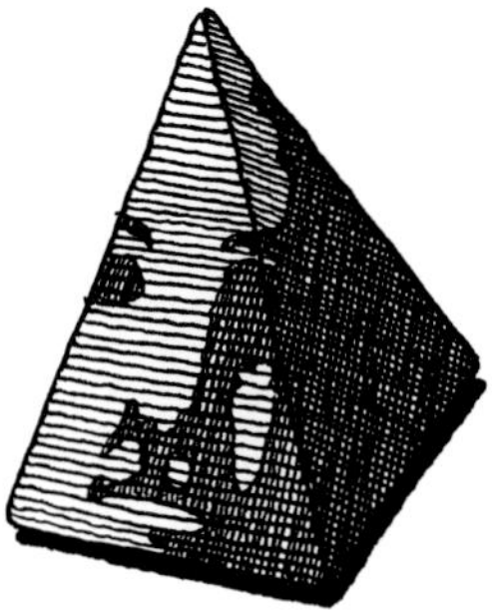

Although Jan was trained as a painter and printmaker, there was no way to make a living in the visual arts in Poland other than poster art. The regime had chosen to support poster art because it was cheap, easy to produce, and popular. A Soviet tradition of propaganda posters had existed for several decades, so there were ideological and class-conscious reasons behind this choice. In order for us to get a meal on the table, Jan made at least two posters a month, totaling over 150 within a few years. The regime sold them all over the world. In fact, during the 1970's, when poster art was at the peak of its popularity, one could find them in poster galleries all over the world. If we had received even a tiny percentage of the sales, we would have been millionaires.

Although he was unable to travel within the Soviet sphere of influence, from time to time Jan could travel to what communist propaganda called the Rotten West, attending official shows or touring with the STU theater, and usually accompanied by one or two "guardian angels." The regime wanted to present itself to the West as a liberal democratic government, allowing it to milk Western democracies for loans, long-term credit, and free licensing without allowing anyone to investigate its human rights abuses. The media in London, Bonn, or Paris swallowed this posturing, naively championing the "positive loosening of restrictions over intellectuals and artists" in the communist bloc countries. They never investigated the dark reality. We knew that it was impossible to say a word of truth about the situation, for in doing so, our families back in Poland would be at the mercy of the secret police. In short, Jan's trips abroad were carefully controlled exposures of an opposition artist, designed to prove to the West that the system was liberal, while not allowing a word of truth to escape.

A similar strategy was put to work when westerners visited the hidden world behind the Iron Curtain. About two months into my relationship with Jan, Ewa called to say that an important Party art critic was trying to contact Jan about an urgent matter, namely, that an American was coming to Warsaw the next day, and the critic wanted him to see Jan and his work. To our embarrassment, the visitor was to be hosted at a Red designer's house in a villa district of Warsaw. This designer, a well-known collaborator of the regime, was a permanent fixture on the graphic art scene, despite his mediocre talent. We sensed that Jan's presence was needed to show a real artist to the visitor, to the credit of the regime. We were right.

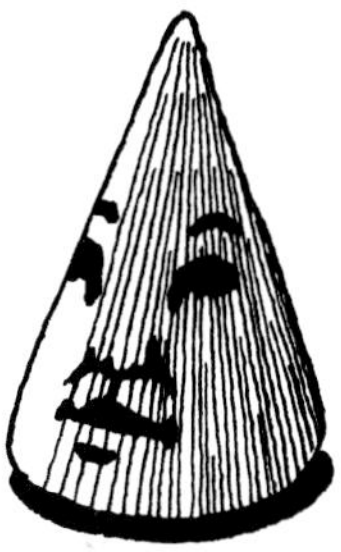

The American, a middle-aged, handsome man named Bob Schulberg, was interested in art and design. He had tried to organize a trip for leading California designers and art directors to the International Poster Biennial in Warsaw that was to take place in June of 1974. The atmosphere and place of our meeting was quite surreal to us, but our American visitor couldn't have noticed it at all. We gathered in the luxurious villa of our relatively young designer host. Naturally, aside from the fact that our host held various directorial positions, including that of art director for the notorious Interior Ministry, he had no art to show. In contrast, my Jan, with his long hair and beard and the dazzling array of posters that he carried with him, looked and acted the part of "artist of the decade," a transplant from San Francisco's Haight-Ashbury. It didn't matter that he was poor and a political liability. For a moment he was "it" and the West loved it!

Bob was impressed by us and by Jan's work and he focussed on what we had to show and say. He was impressed by Jan's candid comments about the situation in Poland. Our hosts were delighted, too; it played perfectly into their hands. Bob thought that Jan could speak freely, and that was indeed true. We could say whatever we wanted, but nothing in the system would change. On the other hand, Bob would leave Poland a "witness" to greater freedom than he had expected. We understood this just as well as our hosts did.

This meeting was a typical masquerade, part of a general communist strategy that used art for propaganda purposes. The famous Soviet ballets and operas, the remnants of a world the Revolution had obliterated, were maintained as glittering examples of Russian culture. Modern dance companies, theaters, and beautiful, poetic films "untainted" by commercialism were all intended to hypnotize the West. The implied message was that the world on the other side of the Curtain was a paradise for serious art and culture. Western intellectuals and artists, many of them with leftist sympathies fueled by Eastern bloc art and cultural propaganda, would visit Poland and other Soviet-dominated countries to see firsthand the "miracle of communism" at work. They were carefully separated from the poverty zones, prisonlike apartment blocks, and long lines for food. Instead, their hosts, members of the elite, arranged such staged events like this meeting between Bob Schulberg and Jan.

At the end of the meeting, Jan handed all of his posters to Bob as a gift. This was nothing special: on our side of the Iron Curtain, Jan's posters were next to worthless; anybody was able to buy one on the street from a "posting man" for a dollar or less. We said farewell and never expected to see Bob again.

Once our American guest was gone, everything returned to normal; we went back to our state of continual financial insecurity. This was a very difficult time for us. We were barely hanging on. Luckily though, during our first year together, a stroke of good fortune would help us to get married. In 1974, I won the national car lottery, which I entered thanks to my mother.

A car was regarded as an almost priceless object of desire in communist countries. Domestic cars, produced in small quantities, were of appalling design and quality, while Western imports were available only sporadically, and then only to the privileged (the Reds, who else?). The price of the cheapest Polish-made car, the Syrena (Mermaid) cost more than five years of the salary of a middle-class citizen. A dealership network was practically nonexistent, and spare parts were so scarce that one had to buy them on the black market.

To squeeze their mediocre savings out of people, the government created the car lottery. Because cars were always in short supply due to low annual production, special bank accounts were formed for eager citizens to save money, bit by bit, to buy their dream machine someday. This, however, didn't mean that one would have a car once enough money was saved. Sometimes the shortages in production were so severe that an already-paid-for car would arrive three years behind schedule, and at three times the original price.

When my sisters and I were six years old, mother opened accounts for us in the hope that one day one of us would win the car lottery. Several people—maybe a hundred—won annually. To my surprise, one day Mom telephoned with the good news: I had won my Mermaid! After several days of bureaucratic paperwork, Jan and I went to Katowice, the Silesian province capital, some 200 miles from Warsaw, to collect our prize. The idea was to sell the monster right away, for we were not interested in owning such a machine. Gas prices were exorbitant, plus the Mermaid was a true remnant of the Ice Age that had somehow outlived the woolly mammoth. Our friends informed us that we would be able to sell it quickly to fans hovering around the parking lot.

All available cars were in an already fading turquoise, with some scratches here and there. Nobody complained, for after all, the engine was still in place. The car smelled like a tractor, the steering wheel stuck out of the primitive dashboard like in a bumper car in an amusement park, and the necessary "spares" plus a can of turquoise paint were locked in the trunk. The potential buyers crowded around us instantly. Not knowing that we could have charged far more than the factory invoice, we sold the car in the blink of an eye. We wanted to get rid of it and head back to Warsaw as soon as possible.

We returned half of the booty to my mother, for it was her money and sweat that had paid us so handsomely. We were happy, for there was enough left to pay for another year of rent, and to buy the wedding rings for our upcoming big event. The purchase of the wedding rings was also a stroke of luck. One couldn't just go out and buy wedding rings back then. I happened to be passing by a long line when I learned that wedding rings had suddenly appeared at the store. I immediately queued up, and more luck, I happened to have a relatively large sum of money in my purse. Wedding rings cost as much as an entire month of living expenses. Obviously it was meant to be!

We decided to marry in December of 1974, roughly a year after we had met. First we underwent the obligatory civil wedding. Jan painted my wedding dress. It didn't dry in time for the ceremony, so we had to stand on the bus on the way to the clerk's office. There were only six people present. Ewa was my witness, while Jan's witness was his great friend, Jonasz Kofta, an outstanding poet and cabaret actor. To make the scene complete, our marriage took place at the municipal building across from the notorious Rakowiecka Street prison complex used for political trials. To us it wouldn't have made any difference had we been in Siberia or a tropical jungle. More colorful still, was the clerk who married us: he was rather toothless, lisped, and was completely drunk. Our guests and witnesses could barely contain their laughter! Jan and I, however, were deadly serious; we both knew that this was a big moment in our lives.

My mother organized our church wedding ceremony to be held just after Christmas of the same year, December 26, 1974. It took place in Częstochowa, of course. The reception was held at Mom's apartment, and even my estranged father was invited. Afterwards, we went to Krościenko in the Pieniny Mountains, the very place where only a year ago I had met Jan's father, sister, and Ares, the dog. At the end of a weeklong stay, I started to have all the symptoms of being pregnant. We were shocked, especially because the family doctor who had prescribed my contraceptives had assured me that I was 125 percent secure.

When I visited the doctor, he was amazed. I was indeed pregnant. He glanced at Jan admiringly, as if he were a man that no contraceptive could hold back! After that funny moment, however, Jan and I faced a serious issue. We had planned to have a child after we had settled down and secured some financial stability. But now, that didn't seem possible. As with the many emergencies that we were to face in our lives, we concluded that we would cope with the situation. Jan dreamed to have a daughter, despite all of his friends' wishes for a boy.

This was a terribly difficult time to be pregnant. While I was expecting, we were forced to move three times, as Jan was legally forbidden to live anywhere. Nevertheless, I managed to continue my studies in psychology.

Luckily, people within the Party and of influence in the art world began to help us quietly, making up for a system intent on destroying individual expression. Censorship, the closing of exhibitions and plays, and restrictions on travel and movement were tactics commonly used to undermine careers.

Some sympathetic people in the National Museums designated Jan to represent Poland in the International Festival of Painting (1975) in Cagnes-sur-Mer, France. Another person who decided to support us discreetly was Konstanty Węgrzyn from the Ministry of Culture. Coming from Cracow, he knew and admired Jan's work with the STU Theater. Węgrzyn awarded my husband a major artist's stipend to prepare for the Cagnes-sur-Mer Competition of Painting. Those who helped us could have faced serious consequences by supporting an artist who openly opposed the Party. Had it not been for a very important turn of events in Cagnes-sur-Mer, those who stood behind Jan would have lost their jobs and positions, at the very least.

Just a month before the birth of our child, Jan and I miraculously obtained permission from the government to attend the French festival—they probably hoped they would never see us again. There, Jan won the top awards, the Oscar de la Peinture and the President's Award. It was a crucial break in our lives, one that brought him recognition in the international art scene. We knew to use this brief moment to escape the limbo in which the regime was carefully keeping us. As a result of the awards, Jan was invited by the Pompidou Center in Paris to do a residency.

We returned to Warsaw where another paradox awaited us. In any other system, Jan would have been pampered after winning a prestigious art prize abroad, but in Poland he was practically ostracized. It was quickly made obvious to us that the Party felt that the award had gone to the "wrong" person—it should have been given to the Party's favorite. Jan lost almost all his commissions and we were desperately poor. Mother helped us immensely, loaning us money and regularly travelling three hours by train from Częstochowa, carrying food that her patients had helped her to find. Ironically, at the same time, his theatrical and Jazz Series posters decorated the walls of hip young people from Frankfurt to Berkeley.

Our baby girl was born in August. We were elated. Imagine Jan's joy—he got his dream in the flesh, crying with the force of a hurricane! I continued to study full time. Together we took care of our child, whom we named Hanna, after me. Had it been a boy, we would have named him Jan.

The Cagnes-sur-Mer award started opening doors for us. The curators of the Pompidou Center began a drive to invite Jan to Paris for a two-year stay, and international art critics and artists began to recognize him as a great talent worthy of further support. In Polish art circles many uncorrupted critics and museum curators voiced the same support in defiance of the regime. On the one hand, Jan was an asset for the Polish propaganda machine directed toward the West; on the other hand, he was a cult figure in the flourishing, dangerous counter-culture of Poland.

Our financial situation was worsening, and we could feel the officials trying to break our resolve to be independent. They were trying to force us into signing a pact with the devil, as many friends had done out of despair. This pact was a verbal or written agreement in which an artist, writer, journalist, professor, or other person working in art or culture, promised to cease political activity and the support of individuals not endorsed, whether openly or quietly, by the Party. In return, one was guaranteed a quiet and secure life, a passport, and limited and controlled access to exhibitions, publications, or whatever was the arena of one's activities.

Jan started to fight to get an exit visa for the entire family to go to Paris, as the French curators had proposed. The Ministry of Culture in Warsaw was more than uncooperative and in the span of five months Jan was rebuffed three times. The situation looked quite desperate.

Jan was increasingly regarded as an outcast as he tried to gain official leave. Commissions dried up completely, and our circle of friends shrank dramatically, for a lot of people were too afraid to be identified with us anymore. I endured long hours of uncertainty when Jan was at the Ministry seeing about our exit visas. I recalled the terrible stories of people who had never returned from such visits.

In the meantime, a new element was added to our international dealings. Thanks to the pressure of French curators and the Japanese graphic designer Shigeo Fukuda, whom we had met in Warsaw in 1974 at the International Poster Biennial, Jan was invited as a special guest to the International Design Conference in Aspen, Colorado. This prestigious conference would be a particularly exceptional event in 1976, as it was the year of the American bicentennial. We never received the invitation personally; presumably, it was intercepted by the Polish secret police (a very normal procedure). Luckily, the American Embassy in Warsaw had already intervened at the Ministry of Culture on Jan's behalf. This happened in February of 1976.

Yet another event fired our emotions. A curator at the renowned Wilanów Poster Museum in Warsaw, Janina Fijałkowska, got permission through official channels to organize a show of Polish poster designers. Generally speaking, censors never allowed artworks to be shown in a prestigious museum without screening each piece, but officials in this case were not particularly concerned. They assumed that the designers would only exhibit posters, which were always censored before printing in tightly controlled state facilities. The "poster designers" in question, however, were artists working in a broad array of media, including paintings, prints, and set designs, and the show included the full range of works. In addition, no one told the officials that the artists were Jan and his three close friends, Jan Aleksiun, Eugeniusz Stankiewicz, and Jerzy Czerniawski, known as "The Four." Besides being known as rebels of the Polish School of Poster Design, The Four were undisputed stars of Polish art and design, and they were young, ranging from twenty-seven to thirty-five years old. When the big show opened in March of that same year, it included brilliant and controversial paintings and prints never before publicly displayed or censored.

The show was an instant sensation and an embarrassment for officialdom. The quality and range of the exhibition was so outstanding that foreign museums expressed interest in hosting the show after Warsaw. The public poured into the museum by the thousands. The regime immediately banned television coverage of the show and tried to quell the growing interest and controversy, but it was too late.

The show of The Four helped us immensely to obtain our exit visas. The Party squarely blamed Jan as the leader of the group. To them, he was the man who had manipulated the whole situation into being. They wanted to get rid of him before he made more trouble.

One week after the show ended, the Ministry of Culture summoned Jan and informed him that we would be granted our visas. An ugly confrontation with the deputy Minister of Culture culminated with the angry warning that Jan was not welcome anymore in socialist Poland and should take all his works with him. This was another incredible stroke of luck. Normally the customs office was very reluctant to allow the exportation of even contemporary artworks, including the personal works of living artists.

It is highly probable that the regime's plan was to get Jan out of Poland, where he had become a figure too powerful to destroy, without raising public protest. People in the ministry placed their bets on sending Jan to the West where, everyone believed, an artist from behind the Iron Curtain could never make it without the support of the regime and its friends. They must have thought that, even though Jan was strong in Poland, he would quietly disappear in the West. This was not an unsafe bet, considering the huge extent of Soviet influence on culture abroad. The regime could always count on their leftist brothers in the Western worlds of art, media, and academia to hinder any efforts made by someone like Jan. To tell the truth, if we hadn't put up such a fight, the Ministry's bet would have worked out just as planned.

In one day, Jan received the permit to carry all his works out of the country, and three computer cards containing our passport data (or rather, police data) for the customs office. Even Hanna, just nine months old, had a computer card on her listing "dangerous information" about her father's involvement in the opposition and her grandfather's activities in the prewar Socialist party. Ironically, the IBM cards punctured with data were proudly marked "Made in U.S.A." We were terribly scared and stressed, but several friends who knew the regime well enough urged us to leave immediately. They argued that the Reds could change their minds very quickly, and perhaps the chance that we now had was the only one we would ever have.

We packed our most important things into four suitcases. I collected my meager jewelry and some valuables and put them into my best suitcase. The works, in several big cardboard cases and posters in tubes, were sent separately through the French Embassy. It was May 26, 1976.

We arrived at Warsaw Airport at 8 AM, and the customs and border control officers processed us with the speed of light. Mom was barely able to kiss us and we were gone. Inside the jetliner we were seated in the very front of the cabin, separated from the "legitimate" passengers by two rows of seats filled with mail sacks. Little Hanna sat on my lap, motionlessly and calmly observing the surroundings. It was as if she sensed the weight of the moment. I was cold and numb inside, like in a trance. I silently prayed to see us taking off. A single officer in civilian clothes came on board and checked us with a glance, then left. We took off, and I was certain that I was seeing Warsaw for the last time in my life.

The flight was uneventful, but a nasty surprise greeted us upon our arrival to Paris. My best suitcase with my best things was promptly stolen from the conveyor belt, as in a flimsy script of a melodramatic B-class film. Holding little Hanna in my arms, I explained to myself, "It seems that God has decided that we must start totally from scratch." I didn't cry.

Chapter 7

Pompidou, Paris, and Poverty

For the first two months of our stay in Paris, we lived in the flat of François and Arlette Barré. François was the curator of the CCI department (Centre de Création Industriel) of the Pompidou Center, a new art center, still under construction, that had been designated by the French government as a "factory for artists." The establishment of this institution was part of the French response to the inroads American culture was making in Europe, through things as diverse as rock n' roll, jazz, pop art, films, literature, blue jeans, and fast food. It was François who managed to obtain the invitation for Jan to come to Paris. Everything looked bright at first.

Within two weeks, Jan went to the Aspen conference as the youngest guest artist there. Several top American curators and art directors encouraged Jan to seek immediate political asylum in America, but Jan refused, explaining that if he did, blame would be put on the Pompidou Center, and chances for other artists from Poland to leave the country legally would be ruined. We had also been promised a very good living situation in Paris after Jan returned from the States.

At the conference, Jan was paired with Shigeo Fukuda, and the two of them created a great presentation of their work at the general session. Jan had smuggled in a copy of a documentary film on The Four and the memorable show at the Wilanów Poster Museum. Our friend, documentary filmmaker Antoni Dzieduszycki, had made it illegally, within the span of

one day, just before the show was closed down. National TV had not wanted any footage taken, so an official technical crew was prevented from coming to the museum. Thus, the film had no sound. Thanks to this, however, the half-hour documentary looked even more dramatic.

Jan was back in Paris after three weeks, full of optimism. But despite all the promises, matters started to unravel badly. Our hosts left for a vacation in Deauville and we stayed in their Montmartre flat alone and without a dime. Jan worked furiously, painting on paper on the empty table of our absent hosts. We listened to Bob Dylan. The heat was incredible—this was one of the hottest summers in France's history. We were in such a financial squeeze that even one banana a day to enrich little Hanna's diet was sometimes a problem. As is usual in August, Paris was empty, so even a small commission of an illustration or book cover was out of the question.

Thus, I created super-minimalistic dishes out of almost nothing to sustain some kind of a basic menu for us. I tried to buy the cheapest ingredients, like beef kidneys. One day while preparing such a specialty, Hanna's crying distracted me. When I returned to the kitchen, our hosts' cat had just finished eating the kidneys. I was furious and spanked the poor beast; a moment later he peed on our daughter's bed.

This was the lowest point of my life—left in an inhospitable city and abandoned by a curator who had "arranged" everything, with no way out. One day during this period I was faced with a situation I had never before imagined: I couldn't afford to host guests. I only had barely enough to get ingredients for a cake. I was ashamed of the position in which I found myself.

Then, two days later, we learned that Jan's father had died. Jan's sister, Anna, called from Poland and warned us that the police were inquiring about us, an obvious sign that the decision of letting us go had been reversed. Our friends had been right; we had taken the only chance we would have ever gotten to leave.

We were numb. Jan worked on a protest poster depicting a tank rolling down an empty city street. He didn't stop working after the sad news, he

Cinaders (Braised Kidneys)

Serves 4

This is a meal that you can make the day before; just reheat it before serving. It tastes best with rice.

2 pounds veal kidneys
2 tablespoons vegetable or olive oil
1 large onion, diced
1/2 teaspoon salt
1/2 teaspoon freshly ground pepper
1 garlic clove, minced
2 bay leaves
Slurry: 1 tablespoons all-purpose flour, 1/2 cup cold water, 2 tablespoons sour cream

1. Remove the membrane and fat from kidneys. Cut them into 1/4-inch-thick slices. Wash and drain them thoroughly.
2. Heat the oil in a large skillet, and fry the onion until golden.
3. Toss the kidneys with salt, pepper, and garlic, and add them, with the bay leaves, to the onions. Cover, and braise on low heat until tender, about 1 1/2 hours.
4. Make the slurry (see page 179) and add, mixing and cooking for 1 minute more. Discard bay leaves, and add salt and pepper to taste.

just continued with an ashen face, all night. We were close to a total collapse, and something had happened to our psyches. We felt as if we had turned to stone. From then on, we would be immune to all kinds of disasters as long as we were together and alive. I think that it was in this terrible summer that we formed an unbreakable bond. We were sure that our then ten-month-old girl shared the same resolve.

Our situation came to a head when the Barrés returned from vacation and Prime Minister Jacques Chirac fired François from the Pompidou Center in a classic right-left political shootout. (President Mitterand would return Mr. Barré to the very directorship of this institution when he won the election four years later.) Our only ally, who was to secure Jan's grant, was now out of the game, and we moved to a small house in the nearby Maisons Alfort, some twenty minutes by Metro from the center of Paris. Somehow Jan managed to get occasional commissions for small posters and illustrations. Every night he obsessively drew sketches for his dream project, a spectacle based on large-scale animated projections of his paintings.

Three exhibitions of Jan's works, which included paintings and prints, were arranged in 1977, one in The Hague and two in Paris. The Hague show was a big success, and the enthusiastic director of the gallery invited us to come with even more works. We took our almost-two-year-old Hanna with us on the overnight train trip to Holland. There we learned that the show was indeed sold out, but the gallery demanded almost all the money we had earned for the coverage of costs. We were left with two hundred dollars. That is how we learned a quick lesson about the so-called free art market, which was really a free-for-all for gallery owners who knew that we could not afford a lawyer and were thus defenseless. Again we bit our lips and didn't despair. Little Hanna behaved splendidly and seemed the happiest. During our walk around the city, she eyed a green hippopotamus sitting on the top of a store counter. She was silent but her eyes said everything. In a split second I bought the toy, because I thought that she must at least have some fun out of this disaster. She did. The hippo, well loved and quite battered with repaired ears and a patched back, still sits in our daughter's room, triumphantly dominating the top shelf of her bookcase.

In Paris another person played a great part in our life, a very positive one, at that. He was Andrzej Szklarzyk, one of the most amazing people we have ever met. By then, Andrzej was already fifty, to us an old man. We knew he was a man with many secrets and an incredible life history. Andrzej's legend was greatly colored by the fact that he was one of the main characters of Leopold Tyrmand's novel *The Wicked*. Written in the late '50s, this book was banned in communist Poland, but widely recognized as a masterpiece of political drama. Trained as a mechanical engineer, he evaded conformity just after the war by behaving in a flamboyant manner. Posing as a high-echelon KGB officer, he challenged the ruling cadres in astonishing ways.

Nobody checked up on him, even high up in the government, for people feared the KGB too much. One May Day, that most "sacrosanct" communist holiday, he led the official parade, cruising down the street flanked by two beautiful models in a Mercedes-Benz convertible. Andrzej walked a tightrope all the time, a real master of the game. But in the early '60s his luck began to run out. He applied for a passport and, as was the case with almost everyone, was turned down. Using his detailed knowledge of the Polish underworld, Szklarzyk bought a passport. When he arrived in Vienna, he telephoned the same officer who had refused him his legal passport. Szklarzyk knew the system well enough to guess that this officer would be demoted, if not worse, that same day, as soon as people realized that he was missing.

Szklarzyk was an avid reader of adventure novels about Africa when he was a boy in prewar Poland. His dream was to see the Limpopo River in South Africa. Penniless in Vienna, he applied for several engineering jobs there. Finally, after a year of poverty, he "somehow" found a job in the French military industry and in no time was helping to assemble French Mirage fighter jets in South Africa, which were mainly exported from there to Israel. Naturally all of this was highly illegal, for an international arms embargo had been declared on Israel.

After that, Andrzej found himself in the murky waters of the international arms and "classy" goods market. He moved around Europe and lived and worked in Africa. Once, Andrzej was stranded in an abandoned village in the Congo when revolution overtook the country. He sat in an empty villa, by the swimming pool, sipping whiskey and listening to Chopin's *Etude Révolutionaire* at full volume. His mind was frozen, for he had run out of ideas on how to escape from the approaching rebel troops. Andrzej was simply awaiting death to the music of Chopin and with a scotch on the rocks.

Chopin was a very patriotic choice for a Pole in what he thought were the last moments of his life. A great Polish artist who lived in exile, Chopin composed music inspired by Polish folk music. His music, itself a national symbol, was so meaningful to Poles that during two periods of occupation, listening to his music was punishable by death. When Chopin died, the

Russian occupying government wouldn't allow his body to be transported from France to his family in Poland. Chopin's sister smuggled his embalmed heart into Warsaw, hidden within her dress. His heart is buried to this day in a church in the Warsaw Old City.

Meanwhile, as Andrzej had feared, two rebel soldiers appeared at the gates of the compound. They froze and observed the picture of the lone white man calmly sitting at a poolside table with his glass of whiskey. The music of Chopin was cascading from the amplifier and echoing throughout the compound. The soldiers stood there for several seconds like two bronze sculptures. They did nothing. They said nothing. Then they disappeared silently. From that moment on, Andrzej never went anywhere without that particular cassette tape with him. "Chopin saved my life," was Andrzej's comment.

We met Szklarzyk in Paris in early 1977 through other Poles. Soon we started to meet frequently, Andrzej offering his advice and, in some cases, financing Jan's journeys to America. He once said, "I had my Limpopo, you have your New York." We listened to his stories with amazement. How little we knew then what adventures life would offer us.

I was slowly adapting to life in France. In the beginning it had been very difficult for me to feel at home in Paris. We had left a totalitarian country, after all. It would take me many years in the West to cease fearing the police. I also felt at every step that I was regarded as a second-class citizen, an outsider in all respects.

After a year in Paris, little Hanna started to speak in Polish and French. She was a charming, calm, and smiling child. Jan and I were able to take her everywhere we went. She didn't cry, nor did she throw hysterical fits. From when she was very tiny I explained everything that was happening to her. It seemed that she always wanted to be helpful and supportive. Children are always very sensitive to their parents' stresses and problems, and I never tried to hide ours from her. She, too, started to adjust to our new life in Paris.

At the Parisian green markets you could buy whatever your belly wished for. During the winter, one could purchase Moroccan fruits incredibly cheap—lemons, oranges, and mandarins. In postwar Poland, these fruits would appear only briefly around Christmastime.

The Parisian markets brought back memories of my mother telling me about the spices, dried fruits, nuts, and other products that had been available before the Second World War. When she made various dishes, she would comment on which of these absent ingredients would be used, had they been available. I recalled that French cooking had influenced the Polish kitchen, particularly in the seventeenth century, when Versailles was the most prominent court of Europe.

King Stanisław August Poniatowski took a great liking to the light French cuisine during his youth, when he frequented Paris and its intellectual circles. He was often a guest at the famous salon of Madame Geoffrin. King Stanisław August's Wednesday and Thursday lunches became his own salon; on Wednesdays he hosted painters and architects, and on Thursdays, important figures from the literary world. The king tapped into the intellectual life of his country, while also setting an example for others by cultivating the salon tradition, offering a mixture of French and Polish food, and by not drinking any alcohol. These lunches were above all about an exchange of ideas, but they left an indelible mark on Polish tables.

Although I was the farthest I would be in my life from having a king's selection of ingredients within reach, I slowly began to enrich my cooking. I learned how to make French salad dressings, onion soup, and new meat marinades. That is, when I could afford to buy the ingredients. At times, it was almost torture, living in a place where every food imaginable was available, but not having the money to buy it!

French Onion Soup

Serves 6

4 large onions, sliced
3–4 tablespoons olive or vegetable oil
6 cups Homemade Stock (page 234), or stock of your choice
1/2 cup brandy (optional)
Salt and freshly ground pepper, to taste
6 slices French bread, toasted
12 slices Gruyère or cheddar cheese
1/4 cup freshly grated Parmesan or pecorino romano cheese

1. In a large frying pan on medium heat, fry the onions in the oil for several minutes, stirring occasionally, until dark golden brown, being careful not to burn.
2. In a large saucepan, bring the stock to a boil. Add the fried onions; reduce the heat to low and simmer for 30 minutes. If desired, stir in 1/2 cup brandy 10 minutes before removing from heat.
3. Preheat the oven to 450°. Add salt and pepper to the soup to taste. Pour it into 6 ovenproof serving vessels. Float a slice of toast on top of each, and cover with 2 slices Gruyère or cheddar cheese and 2 teaspoons Parmesan cheese. Bake in the oven until cheese is melted, and serve.

Chapter 8

A New Life in New York

Jan traveled to the United States three times during our stay in France. One important visit had been to the Aspen Design Conference. He also went to Los Angeles to see Bob Schulberg, whose family had dominated the Hollywood film scene for many years, particularly in the 1930s. His cousin, Budd Schulberg, is the famous author and screenwriter—among the films he authored was *On the Waterfront*. After Jan's trip to Los Angeles in the spring of 1977, together with Bob, we decided to do whatever it took to move to New York as soon as possible. We were thinking along practical lines, it turned out, for in October of 1977, the Pompidou Center informed Jan that it was impossible to prolong his stay in France. Obviously, the Polish government had asked its French friends to send us packing back to Warsaw. French officials who were concerned about Jan's fate advised him to seek political asylum in France immediately. Jan had severe reservations about this idea.

Jan didn't believe that Paris was the proper place to develop his career. It was no longer the Paris of the '20s and '30s, no longer the undisputed capital of world art and culture. The power had shifted to the English-speaking world, to London and, soon after, to New York. But, we were without passports. Poland had refused to renew them after they had expired seven months earlier. With the Pompidou Center backing out on us, we would have been deported back to Poland, where the delighted communists were just waiting to put an end to our hopes and dreams. At the very least, Jan would have been sent to a provincial area to teach grade school.

ENS
• PARK AVENUE
• ZARRE GALLERY
• THE HAROLD
• HOUSTON ST.
• BANK STREET SCHOOL
• SUTTO
ROWN
• SID DEUTSCH GALLERY
• PRINCE S
COLN CENTER
• FIRST AVENUE
• THE WHITNEY
OMA
• DiLAURENTI GALLERY
• BROOKLYN
• CARNEGIE HALL
• PUS
RAL PARK
• ZABAR'S
• PENNSYLVANIA STATIO
2 935 5129
• COLUMBIA UNIVE
• HARLEM
• SOHO
• YORK AVENUE
PRATT CTR.
• 340 EAST 58TH STREET
• TRIBECA
MANHATTAN

MAN THEATRE
•TIMES SQUARE
•VIKING
ACE
•THE GUGGENHEIM MUSEUM
•MADIS
•FIFTH AVE
•THE SAMUEL BECKETT TH
•WALL STREET
•THE QUEENS MUSEUM
•BALLANTI
GREENWICH VANGUARD
•DORSKY GA
N STUDIOS
•JEAN COCTEA
•RIVERSIDE DRIVE
•STATEN ISLAND
•THEA
TY
•MADISON SQUARE GARDEN
•PA
•CLIVE THOMPSON

Without any realistic hopes, Jan and I went to the American embassy. Jan asked for entry to be granted for himself and his family to the United States for political reasons. To our great surprise, we were granted visas. We were going to enter the United States with visas that had no status (tourist or anything else) and no time limit, and with Polish passports that had expired several months ago! We did not understand how this was possible until many years later, when Jan learned that his name was on a list of people who could be granted emergency visas. Our lives had been saved.

Within two days we had packed all our important belongings into five suitcases. I bore Hanna in my arms, along with two blankets, a stuffed bear, and the green hippopotamus from Holland. We sent our only valuable possessions, packages of Jan's works (prints and paintings), via ship to America. On the day of our departure, we packed our suitcases into two taxis. As I was locking the door of our Paris home I began to cry from fear. I didn't know what would happen to us. I cried like that for most of the journey to the United States.

We were leaving for a new country with a two-year-old daughter and fifty-two dollars for our new life in the States. We were starting life all over again, and this for the third time! I kept thinking, what would that country be for us? How would we manage? How would people treat us? I recalled the worst things I had heard about America from communist propaganda. Jan knew English well, but I didn't speak a word. I had been in a comfortable situation in France, for I spoke French fluently. Now that we were going to America, I was terrified because I didn't speak the language.

Hanna felt my fear and was also nervous during the trans-Atlantic crossing. She didn't sleep at all. Unlike me, Jan was very happy and quite relaxed when we landed in New York's Kennedy Airport. He asked me to wait a moment while he flagged down a taxi. He appeared in something unbelievably huge and yellow. It was a checkered cab. I looked on in disbelief as all our baggage fit into the trunk without a problem and, incredibly, when the three of us got inside, four additional people could have easily fit. In Paris, our luggage barely fit into two taxis!

I went through a shock of sorts over the large scale of New York and of America itself. The streets were almost empty that day. We had arrived on a Saturday during Thanksgiving weekend. Of course, I had no clue as to what this holiday meant. We arrived at the home of Jackie Morgan, whom my husband had met at the conference in Aspen. She lived on East 58th Street, between First and Second Avenues. I immediately liked this neighborhood, because it reminded me a bit of Europe (beside its scale, of course). Jackie had a small apartment, and Jan, little Hanna, and I slept together in one big bed. When Monday came, Jan began to look for work and for an apartment.

We found an ad in the *New York Times* for a furnished apartment up for rent. This was important to us, as we wouldn't have to spend money on furniture and we could move in right away. The apartment was near Jackie's place and the neighborhood looked safe. We took the apartment right away and moved in that very day.

Jan immediately began to look for commissions. His impressive portfolio helped him very much. Just as we were packing up in Paris, four huge articles about Jan's work were published. One by Shigeo Fukuda appeared in the Japanese publication *Idea*; the second in an English art publication, *Art and Artists*; and the third appeared in the German publication, *Novum*. Finally, American *Print* published a sixteen-page article about him. Jan had become a world-famous poster artist.

Jan then met with Herb Lubalin, one of the most famous American graphic designers. Herb, God rest his soul, recommended Jan wherever he could. Seymour Chwast joined in helping us. Almost immediately, my husband began to receive commissions for book and magazine illustrations, and after three weeks he started to illustrate commentaries for the *New York Times* op-ed page.

Thanks to his artist-in-residence experience at the Pompidou Center for half a year, Jan was able to get an East 57th Street gallery, where, in those days, the most important galleries in the city were located. Within a year, Jan had a one-man show at the Heidenberg Gallery. That's how we slowly started to make a living from paintings. Bob Schulberg was practically overwhelmed by how well we were managing. He always was with us during these times and for the rest of his life. Of course, his most important role in our lives was as a replacement for our families far away. He was a grandfather for our daughter and a friend and father figure for us. From their first meeting in Poland to his death, Bob and my husband had a remarkable friendship.

From the beginning of our time in New York, we were well entertained with many dinner and lunch invitations at the best restaurants. At first we were unable to return this gesture, so I began to cook dinners at home on our tight budget. The maximum that I could spend on a dinner, including the wine, was twenty dollars. Once again, I had to use my abilities and imagination to transform modest ingredients into impressive meals.

Baked Chicken with Polish-Style Stuffing

Serves 4

The key to tender baked poultry is frequent basting.

Stuffing:

2 eggs, separated
1/2 teaspoon salt
1/2 teaspoon freshly ground pepper
1/2 teaspoon dried marjoram
1 chicken liver, finely chopped
1 tablespoon chopped fresh flat-leaf parsley
2–3 tablespoons bread crumbs

1. In a large bowl, use an electric mixer to beat the egg whites until peaks form.
2. In a separate bowl, beat together the yolks, salt, pepper, marjoram, chopped liver, and parsley. Mix in the bread crumbs. When thoroughly mixed, fold in the beaten egg whites.

Baked chicken:

1 chicken (about 4 pounds), washed and patted dry
2 garlic cloves, minced
1/2 teaspoon salt
1/2 teaspoon freshly ground pepper
1 teaspoon dried marjoram
1 tablespoon vegetable oil
2 tablespoons unsalted butter, cut into small pats

1. Preheat the oven to 350°. Mash together the garlic, salt, pepper, and marjoram with a fork, making a paste.
2. Rub the paste into the chicken, rubbing some into the cavity as well.
3. Spoon the stuffing into the cavity and close the cavity using a needle and thread or a skewer.
4. Spread the vegetable oil on the bottom of a baking pan. Place the chicken on the baking pan. Cover the chicken with butter pats.
5. Bake the chicken until golden brown, about 2 hours, basting after the first 45 minutes and every 15 minutes thereafter.

When we came to New York, Hanna was two years old. I never expected that this would be such a terrible shock for her, but after all, within a day we had changed her house, park, and the children she played with and could understand. When I took her to the park in New York, she became impossible, as if possessed by the devil himself. She spat at and bit other children out of frustration because she could not understand them. I myself did not speak English yet, so I could not explain to the parents what was happening. I went through hell, as I was unable to clarify the situation to people and apologize properly. From a charming child, Hanna had suddenly become very poorly behaved. I was terribly embarrassed. I would come home and sometimes cry from despair.

With time, of course, everything improved. Jan and I sent Hanna to the United Nations preschool, where all the children had the same problem as Hanna, and they all learned English together. Hanna slowly learned the new language, while we spoke only Polish at home. Although she sometimes protested, I just wouldn't speak with her if she insisted on speaking English. Now, years later, she is happy that I was so stubborn!

While helping Hanna to keep up her Polish, I learned English alongside my daughter. Together we learned while watching *Electric Company* and *Sesame Street* on television. I also learned English in the park, where I took Hanna to play. Mothers and nannies sitting on park benches with nothing to do started to talk with me. The first three months were a nightmare. I felt as if I were living in a box. I could not come to an understanding with people. Then, slowly, I started to talk with them about everything—where I had come from, children, the weather, and politics. I would spend five hours a day in conversation. After about a year I was managing quite well in English.

As Hanna grew, I presented her with a role model meant to prevent her from ever feeling inferior for being an immigrant or a girl. I gave Hanna a children's book, *The Value of Learning: The Story of Marie Curie* by Ann Donnegan Johnson (Value Communications, 1978), and she loved it. Marie Curie grew up in Warsaw during the Russian occupation, learning Polish and history in secret underground schools. As a young woman she escaped to Paris to attend the Sorbonne, but faced discrimination in France for being a woman and a Polish immigrant. Despite her scientific achievements, she was rejected from the French Academy on the grounds that she was female. Despite these setbacks, Curie went on to discover radium and was the first woman to win the Nobel Prize. Not only was this story an inspiration to Hanna, but also a way for her to learn more about where she came from.

After some time, Hanna began to make friends with children in the park, mostly boys. They taught her to play baseball. She was a good hitter and fast runner, so they fought over whose team she would be on. I would try to keep up with them as they raced their big-wheel tricycles down 57th street to the park at 57th Street and York Avenue.

I began to acclimate to the new country, but there were things that were difficult for me to accept. For example, the stacks of books that were among the piles of garbage waiting for the truck to come. I couldn't believe that anyone could throw out books! We had cherished books in Poland and we had limited access to them. The communists loved to confiscate and destroy books, and Hitler had made shows of burning books. Here, I thought to myself, was a place where books had apparently lost their meaning and value for some!

I was also disturbed to note that Americans didn't see much harm in throwing away food. In Poland, disposing of food, and of bread in particular, was unthinkable. To this day, when someone is about to cut a fresh loaf of bread for the first time, he makes a sign of the cross over it. Sometimes this cross is lightly engraved on the bread with a knife. This tradition has come down through the generations. Bread is a holy symbol of plenty and one must humbly thank God that one has it. I realized that it didn't even occur to Americans that bread could ever be scarce.

Pumpernickel Sourdough Bread

Makes 2 loaves

The tradition of using fermented starter came to the rest of Europe from Poland. If you don't have any on hand, allow 3–4 days to prepare the starter before making the bread.

Sourdough starter:

2 cups water
1/2 teaspoon active dry yeast
3 cups rye flour

1. Boil the water, then cool to warm. Mix all the ingredients together and place in a large glass or stoneware container. The container should be 2/3 full (at least 1/3 must remain free, as the starter will rise). Cover with cheesecloth or perforated plastic wrap and a rubber band. Set aside in a warm place until it has a pleasant acidic smell, 3 to 4 days. If not for immediate use, refrigerate.
2. When 2 cups of starter are removed from the jar for use in the following recipe, there should be some left. Do not throw it away, as it can be used for pickling a new starter, which will be very effective in baking. For new starter, add 1 cup rye flour and 2 cups warm water (previously boiled and cooled) to the jar and set aside again until pickled, 3 to 4 days. If you bake regularly, you can thus use the same jar of starter for years.

Pumpernickel sour dough bread:

3 1/2 cups water
3 teaspoons active dry yeast
1/2 teaspoon sugar
10 cups rye flour, plus more for dusting
3 teaspoons salt
2 cups starter
Vegetable oil, for bowl and pans

1. Boil the water and cool it to warm.
2. Mix the yeast and sugar into 1/2 cup of the warm water. Set aside in a warm place until frothy, about 10 minutes.
3. Put the flour into a large bowl and mix in the salt.
4. Add the yeast mixture to the flour. Add the starter and the remaining 3 cups of warm water and mix everything together. Knead vigorously to combine. The dough should be quite heavy and not dry. If it's dry, add some more water.
5. Cover with a damp towel or plastic wrap and set aside in a warm place (around 80° is best) to rise until it doubles in size, about 2 hours.
6. Grease 2 baking pans with oil, and dust them with flour. Preheat the oven to 400° with the rack on the lowest shelf.
7. Knead the risen dough again for 2 to 3 minutes.
8. Grease your hands with vegetable oil and divide the dough in half; place each half in a baking pan. Set aside until it has risen 40 percent more, 15 to 20 minutes.
9. Place the bread on the bottom rack of the oven. Before closing the oven door, throw a few ice cubes onto the oven floor, then close immediately. The resulting steam will give the bread a crunchy crust. Bake for 75 minutes.
10. Remove the bread from the pans and let it cool on wooden cutting boards (or other unfinished wood surface). Do not cut until the bread is completely cooled.

Our 58th Street apartment was small, with only one bedroom. Everything had to fit inside. There was Hanna's room, which also had to accommodate a number of stored-away paintings. The living room was everything else—our bedroom, the dining room, Jan's studio, and last but not least, the living room. According to need, the room would be transformed. The kitchen was tiny, accommodating only one person at a time. This didn't prevent me from preparing dinner parties, though, and once we entertained seventeen guests!

During those times, New Yorkers in our neighborhood often re-decorated their apartments. All manner of almost-new furniture and decorative items were thrown out onto the street, next to piles of garbage. Thanks to this practice, we obtained some great items for our apartment. One of Jan's favorite prizes was a one- or two-year-old Grundig stereo with a turntable. This stereo was always playing jazz, because we loved another novelty of New York—a radio station that played jazz twenty-four hours a day. Don't forget that jazz had been illegal in Poland for a time; later legalized, it was still quite rare and a symbol of the counter-culture.

Small and expensive, the apartment was located in an excellent neighborhood, which was worth more to us than space. When the owner of a gallery intended to visit to view Jan's work, he would regard the address with surprise, having expected one in Queens or Brooklyn. Thanks to this convenient location, no one ever refused to come over, an extremely important circumstance for Jan's career. I cannot count the number of parties and dinners that I arranged in this apartment. People liked to visit us, because they always found a pleasant atmosphere and good food.

It was in this apartment that Jan prepared four tremendously important shows for several 57th Street galleries and three in California. The New York exhibitions were one-man shows at the Heidenberg Gallery, Zarre Gallery, and two at the Sid Deutsch Gallery. For the "Conversations" exhibition at the Sid Deutsch Gallery, Jan made a painting-construction telephone booth of authentic proportions with a working telephone inside. It was downright unbelievable when a beautiful, colorful, full-size telephone booth suddenly stood in the middle of our apartment. Other equally large-scale paintings emerged in sections from this tiny apartment. It was a veritable magic kitchen, turning out large and colorful works of art!

It was while we were living in this apartment that a new member of the family, Champ, joined us. My daughter had always wanted a brother; however, our circumstances did not allow for another child. To give her some company, I took her to the dog pound on her seventh birthday to select a pet. This was during a time when New York began to enforce a law where one had to clean up after dogs or pay a heavy fine. Unfortunately, people's attachment to their companions was often too weak to weather these new conditions, and hundreds of dogs found themselves homeless. When we came to the pound, it was full of expensive thoroughbred dogs! I couldn't believe what I saw!

Hanna selected Champ, not on the basis of breed, but because he was the only dog which wasn't barking when we came in. Of course, the poor dogs were only trying to tell us that we should pick them, but their barking frightened little Hanna. Only the forlorn little five-month-old Cocker Spaniel sat quietly, begging with his brown eyes. Dirty and sick, with tangled fur, he was sneezing, had a runny nose, his ears were infected, and his stomach was sick. But what could I do, when this was the birthday girl's choice!

When the delighted little Hanna and I arrived home, our new gallery dealer, Sid Deutsch, was visiting us for the first time ever. I wasn't even able to greet him, as I had to get our very dirty new animal into the bathtub as soon as possible. After a thorough scrub, the overjoyed Champ, still wet, galloped out of the bathroom and pranced over everything in the apartment, including our honored guest! Mr. Deutsch took an immediate liking to Champ, and he would later always allow him into his gallery. Thus, Champ was probably the only dog to frequent a 57th Street art gallery.

I quickly took Champ to the groomer's for a haircut. When Champ's hair grew back in, it turned out that we had a very beautiful golden-colored Cocker Spaniel. Meanwhile, I cooked up rice with carrots to take care of his sick stomach. I soon figured out that Champ was very allergic to the preservatives in dog food, so I always had to cook for him. Every five days I would prepare a big pot of fresh stew made from carrots, celery, turnips, onion, meat, and barley. Flavored with salt and pepper, this stew could be enjoyed by anyone.

Cooking for pets was nothing foreign to me, as there were no pre-prepared pet foods in communist Poland. Dogs and cats would get leftovers from the table. I recall as a child going to a special butcher for horsemeat for our cat. It was very cheap and always available, unlike meats intended for humans. Although Champ couldn't stomach dog food, he ate virtually everything else, including fruits and vegetables—even raw onions! Always health-conscious, he would not go to sleep at night until he had consumed his daily apple.

1. Dancing with Arthur Miller at the "American Clock" opening in New York.
2. Jan and I with Bob Schulberg under his grapefruit tree at his Beverly Hills home.
3. Jan and I at the "American Clock" opening with Miller's wife, photographer Inge Morath, and Jack Garfein, founder of the Samuel Beckett Theater.
4. Hanna, 7 years old, feeding the birds in New York's Central Park

2

1

3

4

Chapter 9

A Growing Circle of Friends

As Jan and I settled into our life together in New York, we met, befriended, and worked with many interesting people. Some of our first friends were at the *New York Times*, the place where Jan got work right away. I would always deliver Jan's illustrations to the *Times* office, taking little Hanna along with me. The staff liked her very much, and there were often candies awaiting her. A frequent and memorable visitor to our 58th Street place was Pam Vassil, the art director of the op-ed page in those days. Our studio–living room became a festive dining space where we hosted the *New York Times* crowd for dinner, along with others involved in publishing, art, and theater.

In 1979, when Jan was sitting in the Heidenberg Gallery, surrounded by his exhibition and waiting for the gallery owner, Lillian Heidenberg, to return from lunch, an artist walked in and handed him his portfolio. Jan took a look at a few slides and cried out to the artist, "What work!" The artist very quickly figured out that he wasn't talking to a gallery owner, though any artist would have dreamed of getting a reaction like that! The two became friends right away. This man, Richard Corozine, a brilliant painter and writer, became known in our family for renaming one of my Polish dishes. He called it Jim Nanewski, which was his way of pronouncing the Polish name *Zimne Nóżki* (Cold Feet, or jellied pigs feet). My daughter thought for many years that Rich had a friend named Jim Nanewski, until she realized that it was Rich's strange pronunciation of her favorite appetizer.

Cold Feet (Jellied Pigs Feet)

Serves 6 to 8

This is a traditional Polish appetizer. The natural gelatin in pigs feet makes it set into a firm jelly. It is very healthy for your joints, hair, and nails.

1 medium onion
3 pigs feet
1 teaspoon salt and/or soy sauce, plus more to taste
2 carrots, peeled
1 parsnip, peeled
1 celery rib
2 bay leaves
1/4 teaspoon freshly ground pepper
1 lemon, cut into wedges

1. Peel the onion and heat it on an open flame until browned on all sides.
2. Put the pigs feet, enough water to cover them, and 1 teaspoon salt into a pot and bring to a boil. Add the vegetables, onion, bay leaves, and pepper. Reduce the heat to low, cover the pot and simmer until the meat and skin soften enough to come away from the bones, 3 to 4 hours.
3. When the pigs feet are soft, strain the stock into serving bowls (two 10-inch bowls are good).
4. Separate the skin and meat from the bones and discard the bones. Chop the skin and meat into fine bits. Stir the skin and meat bits into the stock in the serving bowls.
5. Slice the cooked carrots and add to the stock. Add salt (or soy sauce) to taste. Cover with plastic wrap and refrigerate until the stock sets into firm jelly (overnight is best).
6. Serve chilled, in large slices sprinkled with lemon juice, alongside bread.

After some time, Jan began to work with Jack Garfein who ran the Harold Clurman Theater and had established the Samuel Beckett Theater. Jan's work involved painting installations, posters, graphic designs, and advertisements for the theater, carefully following the instructions of Beckett himself. Although Beckett never came in person to New York to direct the plays, they were in fact directed by him over the telephone, down to the colors of the lights and split-second timing. Beckett kept an iron grip over his plays, making them more of an auteur work than most playwrights ever can or do. Jan communicated directly with the master himself, who highly approved his designs. In fact, the only posters of his plays that Beckett displayed in his Paris apartment were those of Jan's.

I have always been a great fan of the theater. For me, Samuel Beckett was like the Mount Everest of playwriting. I couldn't believe it when Jan started to work with this theater. Suddenly, I found myself right there, next to the mountain itself! I enjoyed the plays so much, and I would take little Hanna along with me to rehearsals. When she was ten, she saw *Krapp's Last Tape,* the first adult play that she really appreciated and understood.

It was through Jack Garfein and the Samuel Beckett Theater that we met a great many wonderful people, among them, the director–set designer pair, Emmanuel Pagani-Ronchi and Robert Joel Schwartz. We also met some incredible actors, namely, Billie Whitelaw, Jessica Tandy, and Alvin Epstein, as well as Joseph Buloff and Luba Kadison, who represented the great Yiddish theater tradition of Vilnius.

Thanks to the Samuel Beckett Theater we also met Arthur Miller, for whom Jan designed a poster announcing his play, *American Clock.* During the premiere, a limited number of posters, autographed by Miller and Jan, were sold as fund-raisers, and I danced with Mr. Miller at the opening party. According to Mr. Miller, the best staging of his *Death of a Salesman* that he had ever seen was in Poland, with the actor Tadeusz Fijewski as the lead. I remembered it myself, for it was so well directed and acted. I loved *Death of a Salesman,* and I couldn't believe it—there I was, at twenty-something, dancing with the great American playwright himself! A few years ago, still locked up behind the Iron Curtain, I would never have imagined I could be where I was now.

One of the most special friendships to come out of the collaboration with the Samuel Beckett Theater lasts to this day. In 1985, via Beckett and then Jack Garfein, the great British theater director John Russell Brown came into our lives. Spending time with John, who is as much a member of our family as one can be, is always a great intellectual adventure. He represents the best of English culture and theater—a writer, poet, outstanding director, as well as a critic of theater and art in general. John and Jan are currently developing a spectacle called "The Creation," a piece based on Haydn's music and texts from English mystery plays. I have always enjoyed the marathon discussions that take place during John's visits. His favorite delicacy at my table is my Duck Stuffed with Apples and Prunes; he is also a big fan of my Potato Puree.

Duck Stuffed with Apples and Prunes

Serves 4 to 6

1 duck (4–5 pounds)
3 garlic gloves, minced
1 teaspoon salt
1/2 teaspoon freshly ground pepper
1 teaspoon dried marjoram
2–3 apples, quartered
10 prunes
2 tablespoons unsalted butter, cut into thin pats

1. Preheat the oven to 350°. Rinse the duck and pat dry with paper towels.
2. Mash the garlic and salt together with a fork, making a paste. Rub the paste into the skin and the cavity of the duck. Sprinkle the skin and cavity with pepper and marjoram.
3. Mix the apples and prunes together and stuff into the cavity.
4. Close the cavity opening using a wooden or metal skewer.
5. Place a few butter pats on a baking pan and place the duck on top. Cover the duck with the remaining butter pats. Bake for about 3 hours. During the first 2 hours baste it thoroughly every 30 minutes. During last hour, baste every 10 to 15 minutes. This will cause the duck to actually lose fat (it melts away) and to have crispy skin.

Potato Puree

Serves 6

A key to making excellent puree is to steam out the excess water from potatoes after cooking. If you skip this step, the potatoes will be watery and they will not take on the flavors of the other ingredients.

1 teaspoon salt, plus more to taste
2 pounds potatoes, washed and peeled
2 tablespoons unsalted butter
1/3 cup buttermilk
2 garlic cloves, minced
1 teaspoon chopped fresh flat-leaf parsley or dill

1. Fill a large pot with water; add the salt and potatoes. Bring to a boil; reduce the heat to medium and cook the potatoes until soft, 20 to 30 minutes.
2. Drain the potatoes well; return them to the pot over medium heat to steam out the excess water, 30 seconds to a minute.
3. Remove them from the heat and add butter, buttermilk, and garlic. Mash or puree. Salt to taste as necessary.
4. Serve sprinkled with chopped parsley or dill.

Another great friend was Dr. Richard (to us, Rysiek) Ores and his wife, Linda. Like Jack Garfein, Rysiek is also a concentration camp survivor who never lost hope, kept his sense of humor, and his will to help other people. Rysiek claims that it was his determination to fall in love that kept him going as a teenager in the camps. When we met Rysiek, we had no medical insurance. Rysiek immediately declared himself to be our family doctor. Whenever our daughter or one of us was sick, he would immediately appear, medicine in hand. This is a remarkable man who has helped quite a few artists.

Our doors were always open to Poles who made it over the Polish border and into the United States. One day in 1979, we got a call from two well-reputed Polish film directors who were at the airport. They introduced themselves, explaining that they'd gotten out of Poland just to attend the Chicago Film Festival. They wanted to meet us. We invited them and I immediately fed the two hungry and tired men, Wojciech Marczewski and Feliks Falk, and they ended up spending a few nights.

During their visit, Wojciech told us about a script he was developing. Titled *Shivers*, it was based on the experiences of his family when he was young. In talking, he and Jan discovered that they had a lot in common. Both had fathers arrested and jailed during the Stalin years, and as members of the Polish intelligentsia, their families had suffered under the oppressive system. Wojciech's screenplay brought memories back to Jan, and he described to Wojciech frequent raids the political police had made on his childhood home. He recalled how all the books in the house were thrown from the shelves to the floor. Wojciech added such a scene to his film, and he asked Jan to design the poster. None of us knew how much controversy would later come from our chance encounter.

Wojciech returned to Poland and made the film, thanks to the easing of restrictions at that time. In 1980, the Solidarity movement, the largest organized opposition group, won a victory against the system, and the result was sixteen months of freedom. This burst of incredible energy was soon to be crushed by martial law. Wojciech's film was released in 1981. The poster Jan had designed made it past the censor's bureau, even though it had a great big red mustached face of Stalin glaring malevolently over a landscape, like a terrible sun in the sky. Thanks to the window of freedom, it made it to the printers. Jan's posters went up, the film premiered, and just a moment after, the authorities decided to crack down. And crack down they did!

On December 13, 1981, martial law was declared in Poland. This was the beginning of several years of relentless oppression. On that day, tanks rolled onto the city streets. To the disbelief of the authorities, however, city streets were plastered with the *Shivers* poster, a normal procedure before the premiere of a film. Photographs depicting tanks on the streets, behind

which were posters emblazoned with Stalin's face, immediately made it to the Western press. What could be better for the opposition and worse for the Party on the first day of this crackdown than for such images to be on the streets!

The next several years were marked by incredible governmental control in Poland. We found ourselves cut off from our family. Mother, who had visited us before, was unable to travel, and all letters and packages were intercepted. We continued to receive any Poles who made it to the States. This included the film director Krzysztof Kieślowski, the writer and journalist Ryszard Kapuściński, the pianist Adam Makowicz, and the Oscar-winning animation and film director Zbigniew Rybczyński.

The controversy that *Shivers* would generate continued. In 1983, Wojciech Marczewski appeared in the U.S. again, with another film at the Chicago Film Festival. He brought a copy of *Shivers* along illegally and left it in our hands. With Jack Garfein's help, we organized a screening at the Samuel Beckett Theater for the New York film crowd. Because of this preview, the New York Film Festival chose *Shivers* to open the upcoming festival.

Nothing could have angered the Polish authorities more. Just when the whole world had witnessed the onset of martial law, a film frankly critical of the system would open the New York Film Festival. In 1984, we picked up a worn-out Wojciech from the airport; he soon perked up, because we felt like a bunch of excited kids in the festival limousine. The journalist Caryl Stern came along with us to interview Wojciech for the *Times* (she and her husband, Bob Stock, a *Times* editor, became like family to us as a result of that night). Wojciech's film and the political state of Poland would attract much attention during the course of the festival and Wojciech's visit.

Before we went to the festival, Wojciech needed a moment to put himself together in our apartment. He was very hungry, and there was no time to go anywhere or to cook. I looked around my kitchen and found that there was nothing left over from lunch. Luckily, I had just finished cooking Champ's barley stew! This thick stew is based on a favorite recipe and is not just for four-legged companions, so I seasoned and warmed it up. Wojciech revived in no time and we headed out for the festival.

Another event in our lives that related to the fight for Polish freedom had its beginnings just before martial law. In October 1981, the Mazowsze province branch of the Solidarity movement contacted Jan, asking him to design an optimistic poster that would represent their cause. To them, it was important for it to be made by a famous Polish artist living abroad and supporting the Polish cause. Of course, Jan agreed immediately.

Just as Jan was completing the poster, a Magnum photographer working for *Time* magazine, Enrico Ferorelli, appeared at our tiny apartment with his assistant and a case of wine. He photographed Jan and the poster, and then we spent the rest of the evening talking. Enrico told us about his experiences photographing in Vietnam. None of us imagined that this pleasant evening warmed by wine would become crucial to us and to Solidarity later!

The next day, Solidarity members who worked for the National Polish Airlines smuggled the poster into Poland. They took it to the Solidarity printing plant in Łódź, where it was scheduled to be printed in preparation for the coming year, 1982. When martial law was instated in December, the military police raided the plant, destroying everything. We would learn years later that the printers had in fact managed to save the poster, hiding it inside the ceiling. It never resurfaced for years to come, though. When Jan learned of the events in Poland, he got in touch with Enrico and told him that the poster had disappeared. Enrico immediately provided Jan with high-quality slides of the poster, allowing Jan to make the poster design once again.

When martial law began in Poland, the White House, Republican at the time, decided to support the Solidarity movement. They were not alone. The Democratic AFL-CIO showed support for Solidarity as well, making it a bipartisan effort. Jan's Solidarity poster was printed ten days after martial law began, and the AFL-CIO distributed it throughout the United States. President Reagan and the White House purchased many copies, and the Democratic Party also got involved with sales and distribution. Before Congress officially passed a bill to send support for the Solidarity movement (which would take another three months), more

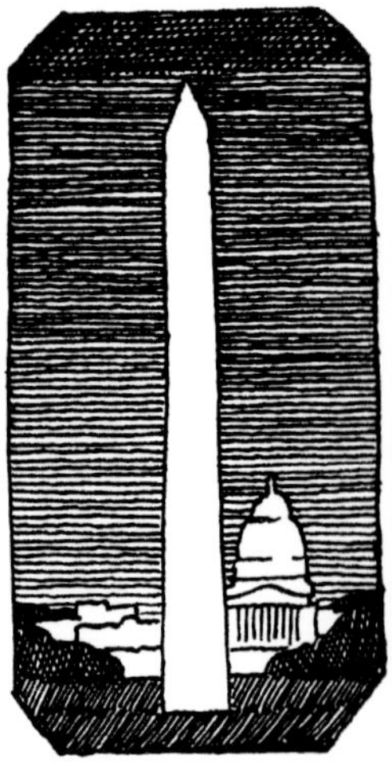

than two million dollars generated from the poster's sales was secretly channeled to the Solidarity movement. We were ecstatic!

One year later, the AFL-CIO organized an anniversary event to celebrate the publication of the poster and its fund-raising success. The event was more than a celebration; it was also meant to remind Congress and Washington's political elite of the Polish opposition's struggle. It was the first time that the Republican party brass visited an AFL-CIO event. At this party, Jan and I met the then vice-president George Bush and other Republican Party luminaries. We also met Democrats Al Haig and Ted Kennedy. We were happy to see such bipartisan support for Solidarity and for Poland.

In 1982, we met James Beck and later his wife, Dharma. James, a leading American art historian and Renaissance specialist, is also an active critic and commentator of contemporary art. He also founded Artwatch International, an organization that defends art around the world from damage, destruction, or misuse. In the building on 57th Street, where Jan's shows were exhibited, galleries would display works by the elevator to lure customers inside. James would preview shows in express fashion, stopping on a floor, looking at works by the elevator, and often continuing his ride down. During one such quick inspection, two of Jan's paintings outside the Sid Deutsch Gallery caught his eye. James was intrigued and went to the gallery to ask for a meeting with the artist.

Jan and James met for the first time in Wolf's Delicatessen, one of James's favorite haunts. The meeting was supposed to be short, but it lasted four hours. James and his charming Italian wife Dharma are now our very close friends. James continues to write about Jan to this day. Dharma is one of the cooks whom I admire the most. They are frequent guests at my table.

By 1983, Jan no longer had to support us by making editorial drawings. The circle of collectors interested in his work had grown. He was having exhibits in L.A., Texas, and Florida. In late 1982, he became an artist-in-residence at the Pratt Manhattan Graphic Center. There, Jan enjoyed the friendship of the center's wonderful director, Andrew Stasik. Jan's residency allowed him access to intaglio printing presses, which were necessary for a project that grew out of another great friendship of ours. Since the mid-'70s, Walter Herdeg, owner and editor-in-chief of *Graphis*, had often published articles and reproductions of Jan's works. They met in person in 1982, and Walter invited Jan to write about artists that interested him. They became close friends and began a dialogue about the lamentable state of modern art and book publishing. This discussion inspired Jan to create *A Book of Fiction*, engravings in Plexiglas that were printed in twenty-five numbered sets of twenty-five prints each, all individually hand-colored.

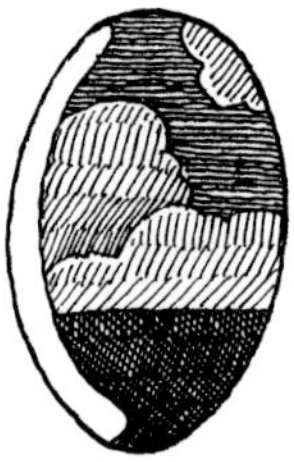

In 1985, Clarkson Potter published an album version of *A Book of Fiction*. The book and the original sets of prints were a huge artistic success. Walter Herdeg became a champion of *A Book of Fiction*, and our friendship with him and his wife Inge grew with our visit to their Zurich home and Walter's visit to us at our country house. Walter became a big fan of my soups.

Beet Soup

Serves 6

This recipe calls for fresh beets in whole bunches, stems and leaves included.

6 cups Homemade Stock (page 234), or stock of your choice
1 pound beets (stems and leaves included), washed, peeled and chopped
1 tablespoon lemon juice
1/2 cup sour cream
Salt and freshly ground pepper to taste
3 hard-boiled eggs, chopped

1. In a large pot, bring the stock to a boil. Add the chopped beets, leaves, and stems to the stock; reduce the heat to medium and cook until the beets are soft. Add the lemon juice.
2. Remove from heat and stir in the sour cream. Add salt and pepper to taste.
3. Pour the soup into bowls, and serve sprinkled with chopped eggs.

When we visited the Herdegs in Zurich, it was delightful to sit around their table and to hear how Walter had built *Graphis*, which at one time had been the most influential publication about graphic design and art in the world. I'll also never forget when Walter, then 85, took us for a spin in his BMW sports car. I knew that we were in big trouble when Walter put on racing gloves and stepped on the gas pedal, accelerating to 100 miles per hour within a few seconds, in the middle of the city! When Walter had roared through the third red light, I grasped Jan's hand. I immediately recalled a Rolling Stones' song where Mick Jagger sings about driving through eleven red lights. We were lucky that Walter had recently sold his Lamborghini!

Another avid collector of Jan's art was Hal Kant, the Grateful Dead's lawyer, who made possible Jan's remarkable commission in 1988—to design the only set that the Grateful Dead would ever have, for their twenty-fifth anniversary celebration, no less. In 1989, the ten-story-tall set, consisting of a composition of large colored banners, was launched for the first time and then toured for two years. This began a new direction in Jan's work, for he began to think and design more on a large scale; the seeds for his emerging visual spectacles were planted.

After so many struggles, we were seeing the fruits of our work, as Jan's position became established in the new country. In 1985, three simultaneous shows took place in three different New York galleries featuring Jan's installations, paintings, prints, and sculptures. This would pave the way financially for our future "country life."

1

2

3

4

5

1. Jan with Walter Herdeg, publisher of *Graphis* magazine, at his Zurich home.
Hanna, 14 years old, with Jerry Garcia during a rehearsal using Jan's set at Madison Square Garden, New York.
3. Jan and I with English theatre director John Russell Brown at a mountain reservoir in our neighborhood.
4. Artist and writer Rich Corozine and I in the garden.
5. Jan and I with old friends. To the left is Eugeniusz Stankiewicz, an artist and designer who was part of "The Four," and to the right is our doctor Rysiek Ores. Jan is wearing a samurai overcoat given to him by theater director Tadashi Suzuki.

Chapter 10

Country Life

In 1985, before we moved to upstate New York, we felt that buying a house would never be possible for us. After all, we had grown up in a system that had stripped our families of their wealth, and private ownership beyond a certain point was illegal. One day, I visited my friends who lived in our building. While there, I found out that they were considering the purchase of a country house. I was very surprised that they could do such a thing, as they weren't very wealthy. I started to ask them many questions—how they could manage and how it was done. I returned home and announced to my husband that we were going to buy a house in the country. We had been planning to move out of our tiny apartment for some time, but we had never imagined a move to our own house. I explained to my horrified husband how this could be done, but then I got scared myself and started to back out of the idea. That's when Jan started to convince me that this was indeed a fantastic idea. Soon the day came when we asked our friends to watch over Hanna for the day and we took a bus upstate to visit Richard Corozine. During previous visits, Jan and I had come to like his area particularly, because it reminded us of the mountainous area in Poland where we had both vacationed as children.

Richard drove us around the area for the entire day, but by four o'clock in the afternoon we had seen nothing that interested us. Our needs were rather unusual, because we wanted to have both a house and studio space. Just before we were scheduled to leave, Rich ran into his friend Anne, who worked in real estate, and she had a prospect for us. We followed Anne to see the house.

When we arrived on the property and saw the huge stables that overshadowed the house, Jan cried out that this was what he had been dreaming of and that we could already give her a down payment! Anne hadn't been expecting us, so she only had the keys to the stables and not to the house. All we could do was peer into the small house's windows. However, after having seen the huge two-floor stables, with its solid 150-year-old wooden-peg construction, we knew that we would buy this property. The big, park-like garden also impressed us, especially as it was in full bloom. Flowers, mostly irises, enchantingly framed the house. We indeed gave Anne the down payment there and then.

Three months later we packed up all our belongings in the 58th Street flat. Richard Corozine came to Manhattan to help us and was surprised to see that we had rented the largest possible U-Haul truck short of a rig. Although we were taking little furniture, Rich was amazed as more, and more, and still more boxes emerged from our tiny apartment. Soon he was in complete shock, as we were running out of room in the truck. These items were all my hopes packed into boxes and suitcases and stored away in our two closets.

It turned out that there were quite a few! After all, I even had curtains prepared for whatever was going to be our future place. As we were finishing late in the night, we were barely able to shut the truck doors.

Finally, we were prepared to go. Hanna waved to her best friend Michael, who lived next door and came out to say goodbye in the middle of the night. Then we were off, crossing the George Washington Bridge and leaving Manhattan behind. We arrived at the house just as the day was beginning to dawn. As quickly as possible, we put together beds and went to sleep in what was, for the first time in our lives, our own home. We woke to the sound of a screeching siren. We had no idea what it was, and we were terrified! Later we learned it was the "noon whistle" at the fire station. This whistle also goes off at all hours of the day and night, whenever there is a fire or accident. To this day, I dream of a technological advancement that will eliminate this aspect of the country from my life.

Jan and I are both city-born and city-raised people. Our paths took us from our home cities to Warsaw, then to Paris, and then to New York.

Although there are areas far more rural, our beginnings in upstate New York were a shock for both of us. We had to get used to the disturbingly silent nights, learn the mysteries of lawn mowing and gardening, and to commuting everywhere by car. This last problem was, from my point of view, the worst thing about moving out of New York.

Our first car was a very used Dodge Dart. This was the first car I ever drove—a strange experience, as it handled like a rowboat. The car was very temperamental, but it got us around. After several trips to the mechanic and carefully observing the repairs, which I found to be the same manipulations of the carburetor every time, I soon learned to fix the car myself. Once, when we were leaving a dinner at Caryl and Bob's in New York during the winter, the Dart stalled as we were starting home. A taxi driver stopped to help us. He was extremely impressed when he saw me—clad in a fur coat and dressed to kill—open the hood, unscrew the air filter, and unblock it with my finger. The car started up right away and floated back home.

In a city, if one finds an ingredient missing from the refrigerator during cooking, one can just pop out to the corner store and buy it. In New York, stores are open 24 hours a day, every day of the week. Upstate, I found myself making countless trips to the stores, which were quite far away compared to the one-minute walk I had to make on 58th Street. I had to accustom myself to refrigerating foods in bulk and to making a lengthy list for a big shopping trip once or twice a week.

Once during our countryside beginnings, I had just baked a big cake when I discovered that I was missing an ingredient for the icing. I didn't have my driver's license yet, so Jan had to drive me. Little Hanna joined us, as she wasn't yet comfortable with staying in the country house by herself (believe me, this was a big adjustment for all of us!). When we returned after about forty minutes, the first thing that we saw was that the cake was missing from the table. A strange coughing-like noise led us to discover Champ, under the table, desperately wolfing down the last bit of cake. His sides were rounded like a barrel! We worried about his health, but he was definitely enjoying a very happy moment. That was how I really learned my lesson—to always keep the kitchen well stocked.

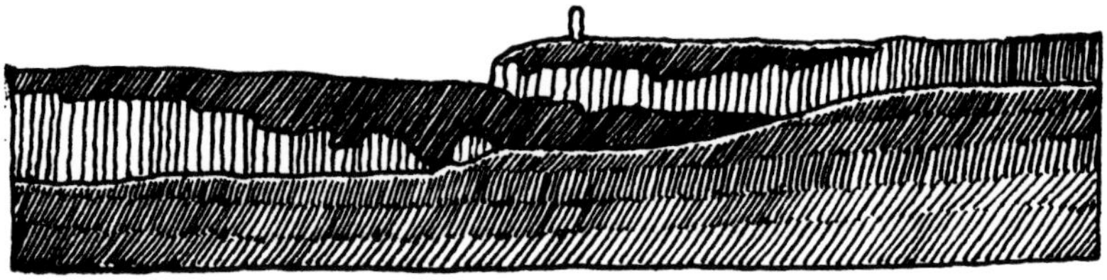

Hanna and Champ, having free reign over the garden, were the happiest with our move. Little Hanna had been unable to go anywhere by herself while we lived in New York. A little boy had been kidnapped just one block from where we were living, never to be found again. This event had filled me with terror, and I never let little Hanna out of my sight. I was like a watchdog. I never even let her go down to the newsstand for the paper. Now Hanna was able to come and go as she pleased. She suddenly found herself in a place where there was plenty of space—forests to hike in, rivers to swim in, and our quiet road on which she could ride her bike. Our house is located at the base of a beautiful mountain. Just down the road, Hanna could go to a lovely creek. Hanna quickly made friends with our neighbors' daughter, who had horses. They would ride horses and, to my amazement, Hanna would even go fishing with her friends and return with fish for dinner! Thanks to her local friends, she was the first to adapt to country life.

I was very happy too, because, after several unsuccessful attempts to find a school we liked in the city, we found that the public school Hanna attended upstate was the best she had ever had. Educational standards were high and there was a large campus on which the students had a variety of extracurricular activities. The school was safe, it had good teachers, and children came from all social backgrounds. I wouldn't have traded this diversity for anything.

The changing of schools, however, were not free of stress. Every time Hanna came to a new school, she met with a bombardment of discrimination from the other children. For the first three months she had to listen to them call her a stupid Polack. I prepared her for potential trials by explaining that things might not always be the way she wanted, but that she was going to school to fulfill an important purpose—learning—and not just to have fun. Things changed for her after a few months. When everyone saw that she was an outstanding student, they had to change their tune. Hanna had great satisfaction in the fact that she had taken it and then, in a sense, won. Maybe these painful moments gave her additional motivation.

After a few weeks at her new school, Hanna was invited to the birthday party of a classmate. We were delighted that Hanna had made a friend. I wanted her to bring a very special birthday present for the little girl, whom I imagined to be a charming young girl in a dress, living in a quaint country house. We selected a delicate Indian soapstone box with a mother-of-pearl-encrusted floral motif. We drove Hanna to the party, and after a long drive down a wooded road, a trailer surrounded by decomposing trucks appeared. Hanna jumped out of the car and was quickly greeted by what I at first thought was a boy. This turned out to be the birthday girl, twice the size of our daughter and wearing enormous basketball shoes. This was Yvonne. The father came out with a beer and greeted us as well. A huge dog, which Hanna would later explain as being half-wolf and half-dog, was chained up next to the trailer. We were hesitant to leave our tiny Hanna there, but finally left, confused. When we returned, not only was she still alive, she was quite happy with the party. Later we were grateful to learn that Hanna's new friend looked after her in school, protecting the new girl from nasty kids like a bodyguard.

Our own house needed attention, as well. During our first look at our future property with the realtor, we had not seen the house's interior. When we went in for the first time, we were stunned to see a tremendous bar, with a stained-glass window reaching up to the high ceiling, smack in the center of the kitchen–living room space. We got busy taking apart the bar and other elements of the house that were not to our taste. The color scheme wasn't much to our liking, with navy blue walls where there could have been much more light, and various kitschy details such as columns and American eagles.

Luckily for me, Jan didn't yet have the studio space where he could work on his artwork. Just a few days after moving, we had workers to convert the stables into a studio. Unable to put his hands into his own work, Jan set to work on painting the house. He painted the entire interior as one paints a painting, with a fine brush. I was thrilled as I watched the unpleasant colors disappear under what was a great, multifaceted fresco! The studio was just finished enough for him to move in, when he reached Hanna's room. Thus, only the doors of her room are painted with clouds; Jan never reached the interior, as he joyfully fell to working on his art in the first proper studio he had ever had in his life.

Our life in the country brought two more members to our household. The first was Arabeska, a stray kitten who adopted us (she had such a strong personality that I can't say that we adopted her). Arabeska advanced into our lives despite what seemed to be formidable obstacles. The first was Champ, who ruled the territory of the house. One day Arabeska dared to convince him to let her in. She brazenly approached Champ, who was lying on the path leading up to the door. She touched her nose to his, respectfully bowing her head. She backed away and repeated this several times. Then she walked into the house. Champ obviously felt his position was not threatened, and he allowed her inside. In the beginning, Arabeska slept on the sidelines, but when she noticed that Champ slept on a blanket next to our bed and sometimes even in our bed, she came one night and lay down beside him. From then on they often slept curled up together.

A year later, a very cold winter hit our area. One night, Arabeska made me understand that she wanted me to come outside. When I followed her, I found a kitten that couldn't walk because she was so cold. I immediately took her to the studio. Arabeska visited her every day as we did everything to revive her. Arabeska had been spayed, and it seemed that she had now adopted a daughter. Hanna named her Clementine.

When Champ died, Arabeska took on his role of guarding the house, assuming his place in front of the house. She would chase away other cats and even dogs. As a matter of fact, she became an outright terror of neighborhood dogs, capable of leaping down from trees onto their backs with claws extended. She was afraid of no one. Yet she also gave so much love to all of us.

Jan was Arabeska's absolute favorite. In the beginning, Jan did not accept her, for he believed cats to be aloof and cold. Arabeska, a creature of great intelligence, conquered the dog, the house, Hanna and me, and finally the "master" of the house—after several months, Jan completely surrendered to her. The triumphant cat slept next to him in bed, accompanied him on his way to the studio in the morning, and brought him mice she had caught. The culmination of Arabeska's adoration was when she jumped into the swimming pool to greet Jan after he'd returned home from a long trip to Japan.

After Arabeska died, Clementine observed something like a month-long period of mourning, respectfully avoiding Arabeska's favorite pillows and chairs. After this period ended, though, we discovered a whole new side to Clemy. Although already a rather old lady, she is undergoing a second youth. For the first time, Arabeska's stern green eyes do not check her activities, and she revels in being the number one pet in the house. The quiet cat has become quite loud and even demanding at times, and she is continually up to something.

Looking back at our move to the country, I must note a big advantage. While we lived in New York, the city was so absorbing that it became the center of the world. When we moved to a place where it was readily accessible but not on top of us, we began to view the world a little differently. The move encouraged us to go to other cities and countries and become interested in the artistic activities there. Getting out of New York opened us up to travelling much more, and it set the stage for a new chapter in our lives.

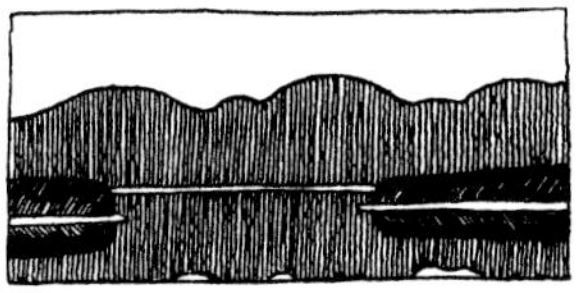

1. An American dream come true: Jan and I with Champ in front of our country home, not long after moving there.
2. Arabeska and Clementine.
3. Backstage: The less glamorous side of making art. Jan and I prepare a shipment of artworks destined for Abu Dhabi, United Arab Emirates.
4. Frontstage: Jan's opening at the Lefor-Openo Gallery in Paris, France in 1991. From left: gallery owner Marie-Francine Openo, me, and Jadwiga Koukou-Chanska, a film producer and a friend from our late '70s sojourn in Paris.

1

2

3

4

1

2

3

4

5

1. Jan's studio.
2. The house and garden.
3. Hanna's room.
4. The dining room with Jan's decor.
5. The living room with Jan's decor.
6. The interior of Jan's studio.

6

Chapter 11

Travels with the Artist

Before communism fell in Poland, our opposition activities made travel anywhere outside the U.S. something that we had to approach with caution. In 1988, however, Jan and his exhibition were invited to the Art, Design, and Society Symposium held in Aosta, a Northern Italian city nestled in the Alps.

When we arrived, we soon sensed that our Italian hosts had strong pro-communist sentiments. The regime was still alive and actively oppressing our countrymen, but we did our best not to provoke any discussions or unpleasant moments with our hosts. At the dinner held the evening before the symposium opening, however, we saw that the Polish consul to Milan and his wife had been invited. We explained to one of our Italian hosts that his presence was offensive to us, but as long as he didn't represent us tomorrow at Jan's opening, we would tolerate it. We were promised that nothing of the sort would happen. As we learned later, the Polish consul had been instructed from Warsaw to curry favor with us. The regime was feeling its downfall to be imminent and wanted to get the support of people such as Jan.

Unfortunately, the next day, at the opening of Jan's exposition, it was the consul who came out to introduce Jan as a great Polish artist representing Poland. Jan had in fact come representing the United States. I really almost had a heart attack as I stood there and watched. This man also represented the greatest tragedy I had gone through in my life, which had occurred eleven months earlier.

Three days before Christmas, in 1987, my mother was murdered in her apartment. The attempts of the police to cover up traces of the crime made it obvious that this was a politically related event. The system was getting back at us for our activities. For ten days after, a prosecutor still hadn't been selected for the case, something that was normally handled immediately. Her apartment was not accessible to my family for the three weeks that followed her death. When my sisters entered the looted flat, no traces of the murder remained. In addition, articles in the press appeared alleging that my deeply religious mother, who had worked as a doctor for forty years and was loved by her patients, was herself to blame for her demise, having had connections to the underworld.

All of this came back to me as the consul calmly spoke to the audience and television cameras broadcasting the event live. Jan could see that I was about to go insane, and he whispered to me to stay calm, that he would do something about it. When the consul finished, my husband came forward. Jan stated that he was very saddened by the fact that a representative of the regime that was oppressing Poland as a proxy for Moscow was representing him and welcoming him to Italy. He pointed to the Solidarity poster that was displayed behind him and said that the consul, a Moscow puppet and criminal, represented the system that was destroying Solidarity and instating martial law. Jan ended his speech by adding that just eleven months ago, the government that the consul so proudly represented was probably responsible for the murder of his wife's mother and its cover-up. All hell broke loose at this moment, with the Italian director struggling to calm down the Polish consul and his wife, while the journalists sought to align themselves with Jan. Italian television carried a special live interview with Jan immediately. The chaos was aired on the evening news. And I fell in love with my husband yet again.

The next day, we found that we were heroes of sorts in Aosta. As we walked around the city, people waved, smiled, and drivers blinked their car lights to us. The waiters in restaurants wouldn't let us tip them, and everyone was so nice. This helped us to feel much better after the incredibly stressful opening.

We met two wonderful artists, Flavio Casale and his son Mauricio, who showed us beautiful places in Aosta. We remain friends with Mauricio, a very talented designer and artist, to this day. Flavio, a painter and a man of great charm and erudition, died several years ago.

I was enchanted by the beauty, aesthetics, and traditions of Northern Italy. Not to mention the incredible food! It reminded me of the Italian influence on Polish cooking. During the Renaissance, an important Polish king, Kazimierz the Great, married Bona of the great Italian ruling family, the Sforzas. Queen Bona encouraged a lively exchange, bringing artists and architects from Italy to Poland. She enriched the kitchen as well, introducing vegetables in great variety—parsnips, potatoes, carrots, and leeks—to Poland. To this day, the vegetables that are used as a base in soups and stocks are called the "Italian mixture."

Tomatoes Stuffed with Vegetable Salad

Serves 6

Tip: Tomatoes spoil quickly if they are refrigerated and stored in plastic. Store them in bags, or better yet, use them fresh.

1 parsnip, peeled
2 celery roots, washed and peeled
3 carrots, peeled
1 cup green peas
2 hard-boiled eggs
1 medium onion, diced
2 brine pickles, diced
2 apples, peeled, cored, and diced
1/2 cup mayonnaise
Salt and freshly ground pepper, to taste
6 medium tomatoes
Lettuce leaves, for serving

1. Steam or boil the parsnip, celery roots, carrots, and peas until just soft. When they're cool enough to handle, dice them. Dice the eggs.
2. Place the vegetables in a large bowl; add the eggs, onion, pickles, apples, mayonnaise, and salt and pepper to taste. Mix well.
3. Core the tomatoes and remove the seeds, making enough room for the stuffing. Divide the vegetable salad among the tomatoes.
4. Spread the lettuce leaves on a serving platter and arrange the stuffed tomatoes on top.

The following year, 1989, the communist regime in Poland fell, setting off a chain of events in Eastern Europe. How my mother had wanted to see this happen, and how close she came to the reality. Jan and I couldn't believe how quickly it happened! We had always thought that Hanna would not see her homeland until she was fully grown, and maybe with children of her own. In 1990, we took her, at 15, along on a triumphal tour of Poland and what was then still Czechoslovakia. We couldn't believe how lucky we were, to be able to show our daughter where we came from.

Another wonderful thing happened when Jan participated in the Brno Graphic Art Biennial in Czechoslovakia that year. Many artists and opposition people invited by President Vaclav Havel came to meet Jan to thank him for his activities over the years. During this emotional meeting, we were given gifts, one of which was a Romanian flag with the communist crest ripped out of its center, an authentic remnant from the revolution there.

I will never forget our train journey from Prague to Warsaw. We took a sleeping car, but it was difficult for us to sleep—this was a big moment. It was the first time that Hanna would be in Poland since she was a baby. She woke up at dawn, staring intensely out of the window at the poor country's rural landscape. She saw a tall building in the distance and asked us what it was. It was the Russian-style Palace of Culture, the main skyscraper on the Warsaw horizon for many years and a symbol of the communist era.

In Warsaw, my daughter found herself for the first time in an environment where everyone spoke Polish. She was thrilled that she could communicate freely. While the trip was joyful for us, it also brought back painful memories. Many things reminded me of my mother. I was able to visit her grave in the Wilanów cemetery in Warsaw for the first time; attending the funeral after her murder had been impossible.

Between 1991 and 1993, Jan's huge retrospective exhibition, "The Returns" toured all the National Museums of Poland. Jan was honored to have his show curated by the Minister of Culture of a free Poland, Duke Marek Rostworowski. This man, God rest his soul, was from an old aristocratic family that the Nazis, and later the communists, had done much to destroy. "The Returns" opened in Cracow. The Warsaw leg of the museum tour was curated by another great friend,

Janinina Fijałkowska; may God rest her soul as well. She had been key to the controversial exhibition of The Four at the Wilanów Poster Museum in 1976, the occasion that had provoked our departure from Poland. It was a triumph for us to be reunited, this time in a liberated country.

While "The Returns" was on exhibit we visited many cities and, of course, restaurants. The rebirth that was taking place in Polish cuisine impressed me. When Poles regained access to vast selections of ingredients, a veritable renaissance occurred in the cooking. Through the centuries, Polish cooking has been influenced by the cuisines of other nations, just as it had influenced its neighbors' cooking. Sad to say, foreign influences often came through war and occupation. For example, steak tartar is enormously popular in Poland. This spiced, raw, ground-meat appetizer came to us during the Tartar invasions of Poland in the thirteenth century. The Tartars also brought kasha, a healthy grain that is very popular in Poland to this day.

Tartar

Serves 4

Fresh meat is essential for this recipe. In addition, I recommend organic beef or beef from a small reputable producer. For further quality control, you can grind the beef yourself from a single cut of meat, or have your butcher grind it to order. Do not serve leftover tartar. Anything that is not eaten immediately should be discarded. Made and consumed fresh, it is a delightful treat!

1 pound very fresh ground beef tenderloin
1 egg (wash eggshell well before breaking egg, to avoid salmonella!)
1/2 cup olive oil
3 cucumbers pickled in brine, diced
1 medium onion, diced
2–3 tablespoons soy sauce
1/2 teaspoon freshly ground pepper
2 sardines, minced (optional)

Mix all of the ingredients thoroughly. Serve immediately and eat immediately with bread, toast or crackers.

Kasha

Serves 6

This is a traditional Polish accompaniment to Beef Rolades (page 220), Hungarian Goulash (page 248), Braised Brisket (page 222), or other meats with sauces. Kasha, a grain also known as buckwheat groats, is available at health or kosher food stores, and in kosher food aisles at supermarkets. Light and nutritious, kasha is good for slimming and for a diabetic's diet.

2 cups water
1 boullion cube
2 tablespoons unsalted butter
1/2 teaspoon freshly ground pepper
1 egg, lightly beaten
1 cup kasha

1. Bring the water to a boil. Dissolve the bouillon cube and butter in the boiling water; add pepper. Reduce the heat to a simmer and cover.
2. Mix the beaten egg into the kasha.
3. Toast the egg-coated kasha in a dry skillet on high heat until no longer sticky—it should be light and loose —2 to 3 minutes, stirring constantly.
4. Remove the kasha from the skillet and add to simmering bouillon. Simmer, covered, until the kasha has completely absorbed the water and become fluffy, 20 to 30 minutes.

It is likely that the tradition of pickling came to Poland from Asia. Poles pickle a great number of things, from cucumbers, cabbage (sauerkraut), beets for borscht, to flour as a starter for bread. Sourdough came to Germany and France from Poland, which was a European breadbasket during the Renaissance.

Another Polish influence on European cuisine is the tradition of crescent- and circle-shaped breads. In the seventeenth century, King Jan III Sobieski and his army joined forces with Austria and won the Battle of Vienna, successfully staving off Turkish invasion. This was a significant victory in the battle between Christian Europe and the Moslem East, and had it not been won, European history may have taken a very different turn! To celebrate the Ottoman army's defeat, bread in the shape of a crescent (the symbol of Islam and the Turkish flag) was made. These crescent pastries made their way across Europe, the most well known version being the French croissant. The crescent shape also evolved into circular breads. Among these are the precursors to bagels, which made their way from Galicia, with its main cities of Lvov and Cracow, to the United States with Jewish immigrants during the nineteenth and twentieth centuries. Bagels, known as *bajgle* or *obwarzanki*, are sold all over Cracow to this day.

Crescent Cookies

Makes 32 cookies

2 teaspoons active dry yeast
1/4 cup warm milk
1 teaspoon sugar
4 cups all-purpose flour, plus more for dusting
1 egg
3/4 cup sour cream
2 teaspoons pure vanilla extract
1 cup (2 sticks) unsalted butter, melted and cooled to room temperature
Fruit preserves of your choice
Confectioners' sugar, for sprinkling

1. In a large bowl, mix the yeast with the warm milk and the sugar. Set aside until frothy, about 10 minutes.
2. Stir the flour, egg, sour cream, vanilla, and butter into the yeast mixture. Knead for 5 to 10 minutes; the dough must be soft. Cover with plastic wrap and refrigerate until the dough rises to twice its size, about 2 hours.
3. Preheat the oven to 400°. Dust a baking sheet with flour.
4. Divide the dough into 4 portions. On a very lightly floured surface, roll each portion into a 1/4-inch-thick circle. Cut the dough across to make 8 triangles.
5. Place about 1/3 teaspoon of preserves in the center of each triangle near the short edge. Fold the dough over the preserves and roll toward the triangle's peak so as to make a little crescent. Place the cookies on the prepared pan and bake until light golden brown, about 20 minutes.
6. Remove from the pan and sprinkle generously with confectioners' sugar.

1

2

3

1. "The Returns" retrospective opening at the Polish National Museum in Warsaw. From left: The Polish Minister of Culture and curator of the exhibition, Duke Marek Rostworowski, me, Jan, and the American Ambassador and his wife, Mr. and Mrs. Thomas W. Simons, Jr.
2. Wojciech and Janina Fijałkowski, former directors of the Wilanów Palace Museum and the Wilanów Poster Museum, with Jan in their Warsaw home.
3. "The Returns" opening at the Polish National Museum in Cracow. From left: Krystyna Moczulska, the curator of the Czartoryski Collection of the National Museum at Cracow; Bruce K. Byers, the Cultural Attache of the American Embassy; and two contemporary Polish poets, Ryszard Krynicki and Leszek Aleksander Moczulski (Krystyna's husband).

Chapter 12

Life in an Open World

The 1990s was an era of many travels for Jan and me. We were spending a great deal of time at other peoples' tables. For us, former prisoners behind the Iron Curtain, the world had become truly open.

A notable journey took place in 1992 to the World Exposition in Seville, Spain. This was the first serious postwar exhibition in which a free Poland would participate. Part of the Expo was an international exhibition of contemporary art. Duke Marek Rostworowski, the Minister of Culture who had curated Jan's "The Returns" show in Poland, invited Jan to participate. It was an wonderful feeling for us, that Jan could represent his homeland with pride, when but a few years ago, in Italy, the situation had been so different.

Jan began to prepare an installation of paintings, prints, and banners titled "My Europe," dramatizing Jan's impression of the last sixty years of Polish history. As the Expo's opening drew near, however, Polish organizers suddenly informed us that they lacked the money to finance the show's preparation and transport! To our great surprise and relief, of all the people in the world, it was the Grateful Dead who stepped in to rescue the situation. The Grateful Dead's Rex Foundation provided the funds and created a precedent—it was the first time that a rock band was to sponsor a World Exposition event.

Our trip to Seville was delightful, Spain being such a beautiful, fascinating culture and land. Naturally, the cooking impressed me very much, but the most delightful discovery for me was that one could purchase ready-made gazpacho in supermarkets. Packaged in cartons like milk, this refreshing and nutritious soup was available all the time and, as it is one of my favorite soups, you can imagine how happy I was!

Gazpacho

Serves 6

This is one of the most famous dishes in Spanish cuisine. There are many varieties of gazpacho; all are very rich in vitamins.

2 pounds tomatoes, peeled, seeded, and chopped
1 small onion, diced
2 green peppers, seeded and chopped
2 cups tomato juice
3 garlic cloves
1 large cucumber, peeled, seeded and chopped
3 tablespoons lemon juice
1 teaspoon chopped fresh basil
1/4 teaspoon ground cumin
1 teaspoon chili oil
2 tablespoons olive oil
1 teaspoon salt
1/2 teaspoon freshly ground pepper

Liquefy all the ingredients in a blender and refrigerate for a minimum of 2 hours before serving (overnight is best).

Art shows and exhibitions are generally prestigious events, with speeches, elegant finery, and notable personalities. It is much like theater in that the opening is a show, during which an event is orchestrated and one must look and play a part. Just like the theater, it has a "backstage," where things look far less glamorous. There are negotiations and paperwork, the actual making of the art (painting, printing, and framing), and also some pretty hard labor to be done. Sending a show overseas, for example, involves several weeks of wrapping, packaging, and loading paintings, which in Jan's case, are very large. Containers for cargo planes and ships must also be built or commissioned, their dimensions meeting precise regulations.

After a show has taken place, all of these cumbersome things return home one day, often without the slightest warning. A huge truck simply rolls into our driveway, completely unannounced, and interrupts whatever we are doing. A great friend of ours, an outstanding New York–based actor named Tom Nellis, was unlucky enough one day to be over for lunch when, all of a sudden, a truck appeared with two cargo containers, each weighing almost half a ton. The driver told us that he could only give us twenty minutes to unload the paintings!

As an actor, Tom is in good physical shape. He saved us in this rather desperate situation. After an hour, we were extremely tired but finished. We apologized to Tom profusely, promising that this would never happen again. He said that he certainly hoped so!

With Tom touring a play and us traveling, it wasn't until about a year later that he called us up about another visit. He jokingly said that he hoped some lovely containers were waiting for him. We laughed and answered jokingly, "Of course there are!" I set to preparing lunch and the house for his visit. Tom had a two-hour journey from his home to reach us, and it was in this space of time that the unbelievable occurred: out of the blue, an eighteen-wheeler pulled into our driveway, blocking it completely. I was horrified! Life was playing a gigantic joke on us!

When Tom arrived, he couldn't even park in the driveway. He suddenly appeared, coming around the open truck doors. He went pale at the sight of the containers, and we did our best to explain. He laughed and, God bless him, helped us to struggle with all the artwork. Thus, we learned a lesson—never to joke about containers again!

While all of this was going on, Hanna was advancing her academic career. Finishing her high school requirements by junior year, she decided to spend her senior year taking classes at the local community college. Her course load was so packed, she was actually able to complete an Associates degree within a year, and all before her high school graduation. I felt like I was flying to heaven on balloons! I was downright shamelessly proud.

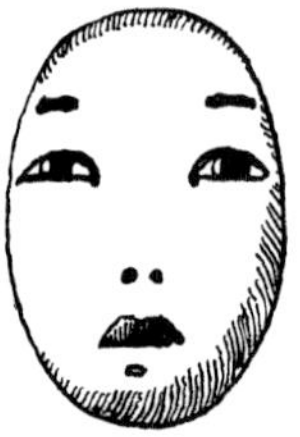

That fall she started at Smith College, transferring as a sophomore. Eventually she would decide on a double major in Theater and English. At first we were shocked at her interest in theater. We knew she had been taking courses in that department, but didn't know just how serious she was about it. This was rather stressful for Jan and me, because we both knew what a difficult time artists have in building their careers, and what a struggle it was just to make a living. Even though she had shown talent in drawing early in her life, Jan never spoke about art with Hanna. I recall being in the audience for her honors thesis project in which she staged an adaptation of the Japanese playwright Chikamatsu Monzaemon's *Love Suicide at Amijima*. Jan was so jittery that for the first few minutes he kept nervously telling Hanna that he approved of her directing choices, as if afraid the whole thing wouldn't be good. But after these first few minutes, the play just pulled him in and he stopped talking. When the play was over, we were both relieved and very happy. Hanna had made a choice that no one could change, because she had found her passion.

After Smith, Hanna went on to London for courses in theater directing. While there, however, she found herself increasingly drawn to film, as London cinemas are many, with a rich repertory. Hanna applied and won a one-year grant to go to the National Film School in Poland. Besides the first nine months of her life, she had only been in Poland twice. After just two months at the National Film School, Hanna decided to tackle the five-year directing program. Since that time she's made several short films, directed another play, and is now working on new projects. This bright future, and the freedom to try anything she wants, would have never been possible had we stayed in communist Poland. This is the greatest gift that America has given me.

In 1996, we traveled to Poland once again. We had left Poland taking with us almost every scrap of art Jan had ever created, in accordance with Party instructions. Years later, when our newly freed homeland found itself bare of any of Jan's art, we decided to contribute many works to the Polish National Museums. Jan and I were invited to a ceremony where Jan made the presentation.

An honor reserved for heads of state, we were housed in the guest apartment of the Royal Castle of Wawel in Cracow. We were very moved, as this had been the seat of royalty for 700 years, during the greatest period of Polish history. When we walked into the guest bedroom, we were amazed by the enormous size of the bed. Our hosts explained to us that the bed had been custom-made to accommodate Charles de Gaulle, a very tall man, during a visit. During our visit to Poznań, another city with a key National Museum of Art, we spent the night in the state guest rooms of a castle that, during WWII, had been custom-fitted for Adolf Hitler by the Nazis. There we found three steps built on the balcony that were made to have the Führer appear taller when waving to the masses. A sobering thought.

Between these adventures, however, a serious event had taken place in our lives. In 1989, my twin, Ewa, and her two sons, Jacob and Nicholas, had moved from Poland to the United States and settled in our area. Jan became a very important father figure for the boys, as their father had abandoned them long before. In 1994, the younger of the boys, Nicholas, had a near-fatal accident. A car hit the twelve-year-old as he was crossing the street on his birthday. He fell into a coma, and all the doctors declared that he had a slim chance of surviving, saying that if he did, he would be brain-dead.

After two weeks, Nick emerged from the coma, but with complete memory loss and impaired motor skills. Although we were relieved to see that he could communicate, things looked bleak. Luckily, Ewa, a psychologist specializing in mentally handicapped children, was aware of how to work with Nicholas and also aware that there was hope. Although it took a colossal effort on her part, she would prove over the next few years that she was right.

We lived close by, so we were able to help Ewa and Jacob work with Nick every day, reading with him, writing, and teaching him mathematics. Basically, the goal was to help surviving brain cells compensate for, and do the work, that damaged cells had once performed. After a year, Nick was able to return to school, where teachers and special programs also gave support. Nick amazed us all with his determination. We felt that as a family, we beat the odds. Nick is now doing well in college.

Ewa, Jacob, and Nick now live in North Carolina, but they visit us in summer and we spend Christmas together. During one of their visits, Jacob made a very important contribution to this book: one of the most traditional components of the Polish Christmas dinner is carp. In Poland, carp is considered to be the most luxurious fish, historically appearing on royal tables and raised in ponds owned by the gentry. The tradition of raising carp continues to this day. For Christmas, I usually obtain this fish in the Polish neighborhood in New York City, as it is hard to find elsewhere. When we were shooting photos for this book, we needed a carp for the Jellied Carp recipe. However, it wasn't Christmastime, and there was no carp to be found in the shops. I was at a loss for what to do. I complained to Ewa, Jacob, and Nick, who happened to be visiting. Jacob volunteered to go and fish one out of the creek nearby. Although he approached the challenge with great resolve, buying special baits, I was very skeptical, for I recalled earlier fishing excursions that Jacob had made with little success. He disappeared for an afternoon with his fishing rod. Then he telephoned, asking us to come and "please pick *us* up." Ewa and I drove there and were stunned to see Jacob with one of the biggest and fattest carp I had ever seen! He had saved the day.

The Polish Christmas Vigil Dinner

Every year we gather the entire American branch of our family for Christmas. This key religious celebration is marked by very traditional Polish recipes. For example, custom calls for Red Borscht to be served with Little Ear Dumplings only once a year, at the Christmas table. Traditionally, the dumplings should be made with wild mushrooms. To this day, delicious wild mushrooms in countless varieties are gathered in Polish forests and sold at green markets and on country roadsides. Fresh or dried, they are key seasoning ingredients in many dishes.

Poles have centuries of experience in collecting mushrooms, but I don't recommend that you do it without proper expertise, for there are many look-alikes in nature that can be deadly poisonous. I strongly recommend that you not resort to your nearby forest for additions to your dishes! If you insist, go to a shop in a Polish neighborhood for dried mushrooms, or visit my lovely homeland someday!

Mainly celebrated on Christmas Eve, Christmas is a meatless event. We call it the Vigil Dinner (*Wigilia*). The meal should begin when the first star appears in the sky, and before we eat the meal, we share a wafer that has been blessed by a priest. We break it into pieces and offer one another best wishes for the coming year. After dinner, we open presents. Really, we should wait until the next morning, but no one has the patience, especially the little ones. At the Vigil table, an additional place is set for an unexpected guest, for you should never turn anyone away from your door or table.

Carp is served baked or jellied. A river-bottom dweller, carp requires some preparation; we buy it live and keep it in a tubful of fresh water for several days, changing the water every day and adding two tablespoons of sugar to remove the muddy smell of the fish. Sometimes, though, people get attached to the fish living in the tub and find it difficult to turn it into a meal!

The Polish Christmas Vigil Dinner

Red borscht with little ear dumplings awaits guests at their place settings. From the center, clockwise: marinated mushrooms; Jellied Carp; herring in sour cream; marinated mushrooms of another variety; Potato Puree; Sauerkraut with Mushrooms; and the blessed Christmas wafer that the family will share. Polish glass ornaments serve as the centerpiece.

Little Ear Dumplings

35–40 dumplings

These dumplings are delicious served with Red Borscht (page 186).

Filling:

2 tablespoons unsalted butter
1 large onion, diced
2 pounds mushrooms, cleaned and sliced
1 egg
Salt and freshly ground pepper

1. Melt the butter in a skillet over medium heat and fry the onion and mushrooms until the juices from the mushrooms are released, about 10 minutes.
2. Place the onion and mushrooms in a food processor and grind into a paste. Allow to cool.
3. Thoroughly mix the egg into the paste and add salt and pepper to taste.

Dough:

1 cup water
4 cups all-purpose flour, plus more for dusting
1 teaspoon salt

1. Bring 1/2 cup of water to a boil.
2. Pour the flour out onto a clean, dry counter or wooden board. Scald the flour by quickly mixing the boiling water into it with a fork. Mix thoroughly.
3. Add the remaining 1/2 cup of cold water and knead until combined. The resulting dough should be fairly soft. Set aside to rest for 10 minutes.

4. Divide the dough into 2 or 3 portions. Dust the work surface very lightly with flour, and roll out one portion to a 1/8-inch thickness. Cut the dough into 2-by-2-inch squares.
5. Place 3/4 to 1 teaspoon filling on each square. Fold the squares into triangles, being careful to tightly close the edges using a fork (moistening the edges with water before joining helps). Take two opposite sides of each triangle and join them, forming an ear shape. Repeat with the remaining portions of dough.
6. Bring a large pot of water to a boil with 1 teaspoon of salt. Throw 8 to 10 dumplings into the boiling water, stirring immediately to avoid sticking. After the dumplings float to the top, cook for 2 minutes—pay attention to avoid overcooking! Remove with a slotted spoon. Continue until all the dumplings are cooked.

Jellied Carp

Serves 6

The fins and tail of the fish are important to the recipe, because they provide natural gelatin, which jellies the fish.

1 whole carp (5–6 pounds)
1 teaspoon salt
1/2 teaspoon freshly ground pepper
1 celery rib
2 carrots, peeled
1 parsnip, peeled
1 onion, peeled
1 sheet gelatin or 1 teaspoon granulated gelatin dissolved in 1–2 tablespoons warm water
1 lemon, sliced, for garnish
Fresh curly or flat-leaf parsley sprigs, for garnish

1. Clean and scale the fish, keeping the fins and tail attached. Cut the fish into 2-inch-thick steaks. Remove the head (can be saved for decorating).
2. Place everything (including the head, if using) in a pot and cover with cold water to no more than 1/2 inch above the contents. Add salt and pepper. Bring to a boil, then reduce the heat to low and simmer. Add the celery, carrots, parsnip, and onion. Simmer until vegetables are soft, about 20 minutes. Remove from heat.
3. Using a slotted spoon, carefully remove the fish steaks and arrange them on a platter in the shape of a fish (use fins and tail, head is optional). Remove the vegetables from the pot, cut them into decorative shapes and use them to decorate the fish. If you use the head, place carrot slices on the eyes and fresh parsley sprigs in the mouth. Strain the liquid remaining in pot and pour it over the fish. Decorate with slices of fresh lemon. Cool to room temperature, then refrigerate overnight. Serve cold.

Jellied Carp with marinated mushrooms, which can be purchased in Polish food shops

Poppy seed cake, pączki, and gingerbread are all very old Polish traditions. Indeed, you cannot have a traditional Christmas without poppy seed cake. Pączki, popular since the nineteenth century, are served on various special occasions, including Fat Thursday, the last day before the Lenten fast. I have

heard that pączki are precursors of American doughnuts, though pączki are more aromatic and much lighter, thanks to the alcohol in the dough. My gingerbread, made from an old Polish recipe, calls for honey, an ingredient that keeps the gingerbread fresh for a very long time.

Clockwise from center: Pączki; Old Polish Gingerbread; and Poppyseed Cake. The shot glasses, an example of Polish platinum-coated glassware, surround a bottle of honey mead, a traditional Polish liquor.

Poppy Seed Cake

Makes 3 loaves

The use of poppy seeds in cooking most likely came to Poland from Asia. The broad fields after which my country is named (Poland meaning "land of fields") are dotted with the scarlet flowers during the summer. Their seeds, however, mainly appear in desserts during the winter months, when the flowers are but a memory. The filling for this cake takes a long time to cook, so you'll want to be sure and make it before you start on the cake.

Poppy seed filling:
2 cups poppy seeds
2 tablespoons unsalted butter
2/3 cup sugar
2 tablespoons honey
2 teaspoons grated orange zest
1/4 cup raisins
1/4 cup chopped almonds
2 teaspoons pure vanilla extract
1 egg white

1. Fill a pot with water and bring to a boil. Add the poppy seeds. Reduce the heat to low and simmer until the seeds become soft enough to disintegrate between your fingers, about 2 hours.
2. Drain the poppy seeds and grind them into a paste in a blender or food processor.
3. Melt the butter in a pot over low heat and add the poppy seed paste. Add the sugar, honey, orange zest, raisins, almonds, and vanilla. Cook over medium heat, stirring continuously for 10 to 15 minutes. Remove from heat and let cool.
4. Meanwhile, beat the egg white with an electric mixer until soft peaks form. When the poppy seed mixture is quite cool, fold in the egg white.

Cake:
2 cups milk
2 teaspoons active dry yeast
1 1/2 cups sugar
7 egg yolks
2 teaspoons pure vanilla extract
8 cups all-purpose flour
Pinch of salt
1/2 cup (1 stick) unsalted butter, melted, plus more for pans
Bread crumbs, for pans
Poppy Seed Filling (preceding recipe)
1 beaten egg, for glaze
Hard Sugar Icing (page 33; optional)

1. Gently stir together 1/2 cup of lukewarm milk with the yeast and 2 teaspoons of sugar. Set aside in a warm place until frothy, 10 to 15 minutes.
2. Using an electric mixer, beat the egg yolks together with the remaining sugar and vanilla until fluffy, 3 to 4 minutes.
3. In a separate bowl, mix the yeast mixture into the flour. Mix in the salt, the remaining 1 1/2 cups of milk, and the egg yolk mixture into the flour. Knead until well mixed, then add the melted butter and knead 10 to 15 minutes more. Set aside in a warm place to rise until double in size, 1 1/2 to 2 hours.
4. Grease three bread pans with butter and dust them with bread crumbs. Divide the dough into three portions. Roll the first portion into an 8-by-12-inch rectangle. Spread a third of the filling on the rectangle, leaving about 1 inch free of filling on the edges all around. Roll it up, starting from one of the short sides; tuck the ends of the roll under. Gently place the roll into a prepared pan. Repeat with the remaining dough and filling. Set aside all pans, covered, in warm place to rise 40 percent more, 20 to 30 minutes.
5. Preheat the oven to 350°. Glaze the rolls with the beaten egg. Bake until golden brown, about 50 minutes. Remove from the oven and allow to cool completely. Serve it as is, or glaze with Hard Sugar Icing.

Pączki

Makes about 40 pączki (pronounced ponch-kee)

One of the most popular Polish desserts, the name suggests puffiness. Eaten year round, it is particularly important on Fat Thursday, when the Carnival is ending and the Great Lenten Fast begins. Plates with pączki stacked high are served everywhere on this day, including workplaces.

2 cups milk
2 teaspoons active dry yeast
3/4 cup sugar, plus 1 tablespoon
8 egg yolks
2 teaspoons vanilla
1 tablespoon vodka
1 teaspoon orange or lemon zest
1/2 teaspoon salt
5 cups all-purpose flour, plus more for sprinkling

1 cup (2 sticks) melted unsalted butter
2 pounds vegetable shortening
1 jar fruit preserves (prune butter, apricot jam, or rose hip preserves are best)
1/2 cup confectioners' sugar, for sprinkling

1. Heat 1/2 cup of milk until lukewarm. Pour it into a small bowl and add the yeast and 1 tablespoon sugar. Set aside in a warm place until frothy, 10 to 15 minutes.
2. With an electric mixer, beat the yolks together with 3/4 cup of sugar until fluffy; beat in the vanilla, vodka, zest, and salt.
3. Heat another 1/2 of cup milk to a boil; remove from heat. Place 2 cups of flour in a bowl and add the hot milk. Mix together with a fork and add the remaining 3 cups of flour. Add the yeast mixture and the yolk mixture; combine. Mix in the remaining 1 cup of cold milk. Gradually mix in the melted butter at the end. Knead well for at least 10 minutes. The dough should not be too firm, but it should not stick to your hands. Set aside in a warm place until it doubles in size, about 2 hours.
4. Melt the vegetable shortening in a wok or deep-fryer to 375°. (If the shortening is too hot, the pączki will cook too fast on the surface, remaining

Pączki

uncooked inside; if it's too cool, the dough will soak up the oil, making the pączki soggy.) Take enough dough and make a round, flat pancake 2 to 3 inches in diameter and 1/2 inch thick. Place 1/2 teaspoon fruit preserves in the middle. Close the pancake around the preserves so that you have a little ball, and pinch tightly closed on top. A tight seal is important, or the pączki will come apart while cooking. Place the ball pinched side down on a plate or counter dusted with flour. Repeat with the remaining dough and preserves. The balls should rest in a warm place for 15 minutes to rise before deep-frying. By the time you make all dough into balls, the first ones will be ready for frying.

5. Deep-fry the dough balls in batches for 2 1/2 minutes; turn them over to fry on the other side for another 2 1/2 minutes. They should become dark brown. Remove one and test with a toothpick to see if you have fried it enough—the toothpick should come out dry. Remove the pączki and blot on a paper towel. Immediately sprinkle with confectioners' sugar. Repeat until all are fried and sprinkled.

Old Polish Gingerbread

Makes one 8-by-5-inch cake

This rich and spicy cake usually has a layer of prune butter, which can be replaced with apple or apricot butter or fig or date preserves. The key is to use a very rich filling, otherwise the taste will be overwhelmed by the cake. The gingerbread keeps for a good two weeks, thanks to the honey. The gingerbread softens after two to seven days in the refrigerator, so it is best to bake it several days prior to serving—this makes it a convenient holiday recipe, allowing you to prepare well ahead of time.

1/2 cup (1 stick) unsalted butter, plus more for pan
Bread crumbs, for pan
2 eggs, separated
1 cup sugar
4 egg yolks
1/2 cup honey
2 teaspoons baking soda
1/2 teaspoon baking powder
1 tablespoon molasses
2 teaspoons ground cinnamon
1/4 teaspoon ground cloves
1/4 teaspoon ground nutmeg
1 teaspoon ground ginger, or 2 teaspoons minced fresh ginger
1/2 teaspoon pepper
1 tablespoon cocoa
1 teaspoon vanilla
1/2 teaspoon salt
1/4 cup milk
4 cups all-purpose flour
1 cup chopped walnuts
1 pound prune butter, or to taste
Chocolate Icing (recipe follows)
Hard Sugar Icing (page 33; optional)

1. Preheat the oven to 400°. Grease an 8-by-5-by-2-inch baking pan with butter and dust with bread crumbs. Set aside.

Old Polish Gingerbread

2. In a large bowl, use an electric mixer to beat the 2 egg whites with 2 tablespoons of sugar until soft peaks form.
3. In a separate large bowl, beat all 6 egg yolks together with the remaining sugar, the honey, baking soda, baking powder, molasses, cinnamon, cloves, nutmeg, ginger, pepper, cocoa, vanilla, butter, salt, and milk; combine thoroughly. Add 2 cups of the flour and mix until evenly combined. Fold in the beaten whites. Mix in the remaining 2 cups flour and the walnuts.
4. Pour the batter into the prepared pan and bake for 60 minutes. Cool the gingerbread in the pan for 10 minutes, then remove and cool completely on an unfinished wooden surface.
5. Use a serrated knife to cut the gingerbread horizontally into 2 or 3 layers. Spread the prune butter on each layer and stack. Spread the Chocolate Icing all over the cake using a rubber spatula (dip the spatula in hot water to avoid sticking). You can decorate additionally with Hard Sugar Icing, if desired.

Chocolate Icing

8 ounces semisweet chocolate chips
2 tablespoons unsalted butter
1/4 cup heavy cream
1 teaspoon grated orange zest

In a double boiler, melt the chocolate chips and butter. Mix in the heavy cream and orange zest, stirring continuously over low heat. Remove from heat and cool to room temperature.

162

1. A holiday family gathering. From left: Jacob, Nicholas, Ewa, Jan, Hanna and me.
2. I am in Cracow's Wawel Royal Castle State Apartments, in a huge bed, custom-made for President Charles de Gaulle, a very tall Frenchman.
3. Me, a triumphant Jacob, and his conquest, the carp.
4. The Sawka family at Hanna's Smith College graduation.
5. Hanna behind the camera on location in Poland during the shooting of her short film "Undercurrent."

3

1

2

4

5

Chapter 13

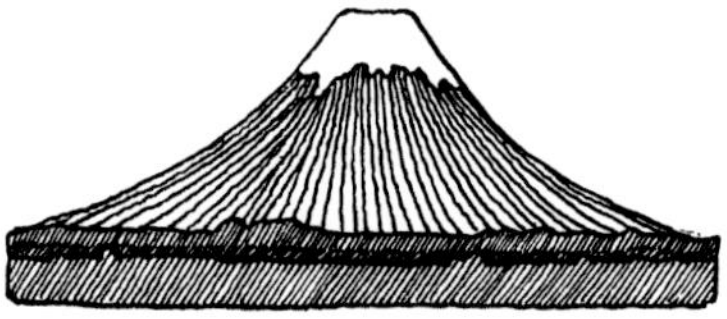

A New Horizon

Around the time of "The Returns" exhibition in Poland, a new world opened up for Jan and me in the Far East. Jan was invited by the great Japanese graphic designer Yusaku Kamekura to do a show at the Ginza Creation Gallery in Tokyo. This exhibition was accompanied by a thirty-six-page article in the art and design publication *Creation*. Kamekura had been following Jan's work for years, and this was the beginning of a great friendship and mentorship. It was also the beginning of a great artistic adventure for Jan that lasts to this day, one that includes theatrical and multimedia projects.

In 1993, the avant-garde theater director Tadashi Suzuki invited Jan to stage a theatrical spectacle at the Art Tower at Mito, an impressive center under his artistic direction. But first, Suzuki invited us to the theater village in Toga, at the time under his directorship as well. Located high up in the Japanese Alps, Toga is one of the loveliest places I have ever seen. It is a very rural area, located in the middle of a great, forest-covered, mountainous wilderness. What makes the village exceptional is that it has three world-class stages, one with the backdrop of a mountain lake, and all the facilities and accommodations necessary for meetings and festivals.

During the day, Jan and I explored the picturesque village nestled in the deep valley. Steep mountains were all around, crowned with incredibly tall old trees that often had a tremendous crane's nest at the very top! This was my first time in Japan, and I was very impressed by what I saw. The houses

of the farming families were incredibly clean. I noticed that drainage systems were built around each house in such a way that wash water was drawn into the rice fields, so that nothing was wasted. The farmhouses were charming, sturdily built, and very large, considering that this region is comparably poor for Japan. On Friday evenings, the entire village would gather to talk, eat, drink beer, and play karaoke. I was struck by an obvious sense of community, and this was one of the things that impressed me the most, compared to the rural United States, where people often do not know their neighbors very well. During the evening performances, although they were local farmers, they became audience members for avant garde theater, too. The Toga evenings were rich with creativity. Mr. Suzuki had invited theater companies from all over the world, and there was an incredible array of work shown.

After this relaxing and incredibly interesting time, we headed to the Art Tower at Mito to realize Jan's spectacle, "The Eyes." Jan had been working for years on a visual theater piece, involving little or no live acting but based on images and sounds. Jan had made a prototype, and he was happy to have an opportunity to try it out.

Jan had worked on the prototype with Marc Rosenthal, an expert lighting and projection engineer, who is capable of working all kinds of magic. Marc and Jan began to work with a projection technique called slow dissolve. Such projections have remarkable color saturation, so much so that they can be screened on water, glass, and various other unusual materials. Marc joined us in Mito, as did two cargo containers of elements for the show. One contained eighteen huge banners, the other a painted palisade.

"The Eyes" consists of projections and then a series of banners that portray a person gradually taking to flight. After the first screening, the banners must float out of a pit and be suspended in the air, each higher than the one before. Once the banners portraying the flying figure have reached a great height, the theater is sunk into darkness and twenty-five-foot-diameter projections begin high above the audience, portraying a kind of journey of the imagination. We had to begin by coordinating complex projections with the suspension of the banners—all of which had to have the correct dramatic rhythm. The problem was that we were doing all of this for the first time ever, and we had just four days before the opening!

Jan explained everything to the theater's technical director, who then proceeded to gather his twenty-odd workers. They then spent half of the day in discussions. Having so little time at our disposal, we grew increasingly anxious as the hours passed and they still had not budged, calmly continuing discussions that we could not understand. After so many hours, all these people suddenly got up and went to work like ants. They worked without a murmur of complaint and without stopping until two in the morning, coming in the next morning at eight to continue. They worked on such a schedule for the remainder of time before the opening. We then understood profoundly what had been taking place during their discussions. They knew that those hours were necessary to delegate and coordinate, avoiding any possible time-consuming doubts or confusion during work. We rarely have had such pleasure in collaborations as we had working with this group. To our great delight, the show went perfectly.

From our first moments in Japan, I was impressed by Japanese culture, art, aesthetics, and, of course, the food. The first impression, before one even tastes the food, is how beautifully it is presented. The Japanese always prepare food to please the eye as well as the stomach. I appreciated the delicate and subtle tastes after admiring selections that were like small sculptures on my plate.

What impressed me even more, though, were the ways in which the Japanese adapt foreign cuisine. I was taken with how Japanese chefs adapted French, German, and Italian food, as well as foods of other cultures, to their delicate and refined palates. I also noted how their eye for arrangement often refreshed a dish that I knew well. One of the most striking culinary experiences I had was having Chinese food in Tokyo, which is relatively less sweet than what Americans know as typically Chinese.

In 1994, Jan met Mineo Mori, an outstanding Japanese architect and designer. Soon after they met, they began to work together and have since become an inseparable team. Mineo, who speaks with us in a mixture of English and Italian, must be the biggest fan of my cooking in the world.

When hosting him, I must always cook more than I would normally, as he always takes at least double portions. He is a particular fan of my soups and was influential in convincing me to write this book.

Sorrel Soup

Serves 6

Sorrel soup is very popular in Poland. The sour-leafed vegetable grows everywhere, like a weed, making the base for this recipe readily available. The soup first came to America with Jewish immigrants, so if you don't have fresh sorrel available, you can find sorrel concentrate, also called schav, in kosher food stores or sections; use one part stock and one part schav.

1 pound sorrel
5 cups Homemade Stock (page 234), or stock of your choice
Slurry: 2 teaspoons all-purpose flour, 1/2 cup cold water, 1/2 cup sour cream
Salt or soy sauce and freshly ground pepper, to taste
6 boiled eggs, quartered

1. Wash the sorrel and place it in a blender with 1 cup of the stock. Liquefy.
2. Place the remaining stock in a large pot over high heat and bring to a boil.
3. Add the sorrel mixture to the boiling stock; boil for 2 to 3 minutes.
4. Make the slurry (see page 179). Reduce the heat to medium and add the slurry to the soup. Add salt and pepper to taste and cook for 1 minute more.
5. Pour the soup into bowls, and add one quartered egg to each serving.

Tip: This soup can be served with croutons or sliced boiled potatoes in place of eggs.

Mineo and Jan worked out the "Abu Dhabi Tower of Light" concept in 1995. The "Tower of Light" will have a shape similar to that of the Washington Monument, a slim needle of steel and a special kind of glass. The tower will be translucent—almost invisible—during the day. At night, it will light up with all kinds of moving images projected from within. It was during this project development that Jan was put in touch with the Toho Studios, famous for having produced virtually all of Akira Kurosawa's films. It turned out that a number of people from Toho had been at "The Eyes" spectacle. An institution that has existed far longer than the art of film, Toho has inherited centuries of traditions from the schools of dance, theater, martial arts, and armor production. Now, besides making films, the studio deals with prototypes and new technology, which is why the relationship is very important to Jan. What is amazing about the place is the atmosphere; the spirit of many generations of great *sensei* (masters) of various arts is present.

In 1997, our Polish past came together with our present life of international cooperation with artists. Jan was key in organizing an exhibition of Kiyoshi Awazu's works in the National Museums of Poland. Awazu is one of the greatest living Japanese artists and, like Jan, he works in various media, from paintings and prints to set designs and public projects. For the museum exhibition openings, we all met in Poland and toured the country, from the beautiful Renaissance cities in the south, to the north, among other places, where we visited the largest medieval brick castle in the world, Malbork.

During our exploration of Poland, the Awazu family was impressed by Polish food, taking particular delight in mushroom soup, made aromatic with forest mushrooms. They tried it in every restaurant we visited, curious to discover the different styles and mushroom flavors. And I cannot even begin to describe their love of sweets. They especially loved pączki, but they didn't stop there. The Awazus bought, and even photographed, enough cakes to feed an army!

Fresh Mushroom Soup

Serves 6

1 large onion, diced
2–3 cups finely chopped mushrooms
2 tablespoons unsalted butter
6 cups Homemade Stock (page 234), or stock of your choice
Salt and freshly ground pepper, to taste
Slurry: 2 tablespoons all-purpose flour, 1/2 cup cold water, 1/2 cup sour cream
Small noodles, cooked according to package directions and drained, or croutons, for serving

1. Fry the onion and mushrooms in the butter on medium-high heat until the juices from the mushrooms are released and steamed away, and the onions are golden, about 15 minutes.
2. In a large pot, bring the stock to a boil. Add the mushrooms and onions; reduce the heat to low, and simmer for 30 minutes. Add salt and pepper to taste.
3. Make the slurry (see page 179). Add the slurry and stir, cooking for 1 minute more on high heat.
4. Serve with small noodles or croutons.

Visits to museums with Kiyoshi were very interesting to Jan, Hanna, and me, as he recognized many Asian influences on various Polish arts and customs, most noticeably on the military arts of the past. Besides traditional European arms, Poles used curved swords and circular shields, adapted from their Turkish and Tartar enemies, who in turn had adapted their arms from the Golden Horde (the Mongols). This style had reached Mongolia from China. Kiyoshi would point out many other elements of Polish culture, past and present, that showed Far Eastern influence.

The time my family spent with this Japanese artist's family in Poland made me feel as if we had, in some way, come full circle in our lives. Our journey, literal and spiritual, had taken us out of Poland to the West and through Europe to our new home in the United States. Then, Jan's artistic explorations sent him even farther in a westerly direction from New York, until he met the creativity of the Far East! And now we found ourselves, families from two sides of the world, both involved in art, eating delicious soup from mushrooms that had grown out of the old Polish earth.

Born in the Soviet bloc of Europe, I was fated to live my life out in a country of prisoners, where others would shape my life for me. Instead, I have seen all sorts of countries and better yet, met people in these places that live passionate and unusual lives. My husband and I shaped our destiny by sometimes making split-second decisions and taking big risks. We have built his career and raised a daughter who knows what she wants to do with her life. Although Poland is not completely free now, with the Red bourgeoisie quietly doing what it can to keep things under its control, I have even lived to see Poland officially shake off its occupier.

This is not a fairy tale but the story of my life. Over the years, we worked hard and I did my best to create a comfortable home to which Jan and I could invite friends and collaborators to talk. Our happiest memories are made up of the expressions on faces and the fragments of conversations that have come and gone from our table. I wish you warmth and joy at your table, too!

Smacznego!
(*Bon appetit* in Polish)

1. Hanna with the Japanese graphic designer Yusaku Kamekura during a visit to Japan.
2. The Japanese artist Kiyoshi Awazu (at right) and his wife and son during their visit to Poland.
3. The architect Mineo Mori during "The Tower of Light" presentation and exhibition in Abu Dhabi, United Arab Emirates.
4. Me on the steps of one of the Toga theaters in the Japanese Alps.

1

2

3

4

Recipes

Soups

I have selected a variety of soups to complement different seasons and entrées. Most of them are Polish, with a few exceptions. Many of the recipes call for chicken, pork, or beef stock, so it is important to have it prepared in advanced. A recipe for basic stock is included here. Another common ingredient in Polish soups is slurry—a flour and sour cream-based thickener. A recipe for that follows, as well. Once you have stock on hand and are familiar with the slurry thickener, you will find these soups easy to make, impressive, and delicious.

Basic Chicken, Pork, or Beef Stock

Makes 2 quarts

Put leftover bones to good use by making your own stock. Homemade is healthier than bouillon cubes, which contain MSG.

2 pounds chicken, pork, or beef bones (you can mix types—use whatever you have)
2 quarts cold water
1 large onion, peeled
2 large carrots, peeled
2 celery ribs
1 parsnip, peeled
Salt, to taste
1/2 teaspoon freshly ground pepper

1. Put the bones and cold water in a pot and bring to a boil. Reduce the heat to a simmer and skim the foam that rises to the surface.
2. Add the vegetables, salt, and pepper, and simmer, covered, 2 to 3 hours.
3. Remove the bones and vegetables. The stock is now ready for use in soups and sauces. If you don't plan to use it immediately, refrigerate it for 4 days maximum. You can also freeze it for later use.

Slurry: Basic Thickener for Soups and Sauces

Slurry is a popular thickening ingredient in Polish soups and sauces. It usually consists of flour, cold water, and sour cream in varying proportions; you'll note that some recipes omit the sour cream.

For 5 cups of soup:
2 tablespoons all-purpose flour
1/2 cup cold water
3 generous tablespoons sour cream

1. Combine the flour with the water. It is important to mix the flour with cold water thoroughly, getting rid of any lumps, before combining it with the sour cream. The water must be cold so that the flour mixes with the water smoothly.
2. Once the mixture is smooth, add the sour cream and mix.
3. Add an equal proportion of hot soup from the pot (1/2 to 3/4 cup) to the slurry and mix well (if the slurry seems to have lumps, add it to the soup through a strainer). This brings the temperature of the slurry to that of the soup, preventing the slurry from turning lumpy once it's added to the pot.
4. Add the now-warm slurry to the pot of cooking soup and stir.
5. Keep the soup at a boil for at least 1 minute, stirring continuously while the slurry thickens the soup.

Asparagus Soup

Serves 4

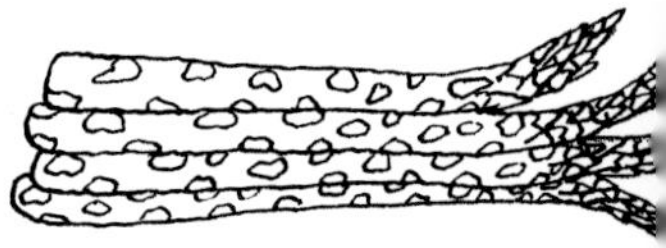

4 cups Homemade Stock (page 178), or stock of your choice
1 pound asparagus, cleaned with tough ends snapped off
2 medium potatoes, peeled and diced
Salt and freshly ground pepper, to taste
Croutons, for serving (optional)

1. In a large pot, heat the stock to a boil and add the asparagus, potatoes, and salt and pepper to taste. Reduce the heat to medium and cook until the vegetables soften, 10 to 15 minutes. Remove from heat and cool slightly.
2. Pour the soup into a blender and liquefy.
3. Heat again directly before serving if necessary. Top with croutons, if desired.

Barley Soup

Serves 6

1–2 dried mushrooms
6 cups Homemade Stock (page 178), or stock of your choice
1/2 cup barley
Salt and freshly ground pepper, to taste
3 medium potatoes, scrubbed
1 tablespoon chopped fresh flat-leaf parsley

1. Soak the mushrooms in water for 30 minutes, or until softened, before use.
2. Place the stock in a pot over high heat and add the barley, mushrooms, and salt and pepper. When the stock starts to boil, reduce the heat to low and simmer until the barley softens, about 1 hour.
3. Peel and dice the potatoes and add them to the pot, cooking over medium heat until they're soft, 5 to 10 minutes.
4. To serve, sprinkle with parsley.

Beer Soup

Serves 6

This is an old Polish recipe, full of the calories people needed in the days before the automated age made work less strenuous. Centuries ago, people actually ate it for breakfast! Nowadays, it makes a great treat for warming up after winter sports or relaxing before a fireplace. I suggest not using mass-produced beer, as there are so many small breweries making excellent brews.

1 cup heavy cream
2 egg yolks
4 cups lager beer
4–6 whole cloves
2 teaspoons cinnamon

1. Beat the cream and egg yolks together thoroughly.
2. In a saucepan, heat the beer and spices almost to a boil, then reduce to a simmer. Do not let it boil.
3. Add 1/2 cup of the hot beer to the yolk mixture and stir.
4. Pour the yolk mixture into the saucepan and simmer, stirring.
5. When the soup is well blended, serve immediately.

You can make a sweet version of beer soup as well:
3 egg yolks
1/2 cup sugar
4 cups lager beer
5–6 whole cloves
2 teaspoons cinnamon
1 pound farmer's cheese, cubed, for serving

1. Beat the yolks with the sugar thoroughly.
2. In a saucepan, heat the beer and spices almost to a boil, then reduce to a simmer. Do not let it boil.
3. Add 1/2 cup of the hot beer to the yolk mixture and stir.
4. Pour the yolk mixture into the saucepan and simmer, stirring.
5. When the soup is well blended, serve immediately with little cubes of farmer's cheese.

Blueberry Soup

Serves 4

Although adults love this beautifully colored soup, children are its biggest fans. The blueberries can be replaced with other fruit: Raspberries, pears, or strawberries work well. This soup is popular in Poland during hot weather. Tip: Lemon juice is great for removing blueberry stains from tablecloths and clothing. It's best to dab it on while the stain is still fresh; this also works for other fruit and vegetable stains.

1/2 pound of the smallest noodles (tiny bows, rice-grain noodles, or alphabet noodles), cooked according to package directions and drained
1 cup water
1/2 teaspoon salt
Slurry: 1 tablespoon all-purpose flour, 1/2 cup cold water
2 pints fresh or frozen blueberries (can be replaced by 4–5 cups of another fruit)
2 tablespoons lemon juice
1 tablespoon sugar
3 heaping tablespoons sour cream, plus more for garnish

eberry Soup, artfully nished with sour cream

1. Bring 1 cup of water to a boil with 1/2 teaspoon of salt.
2. Meanwhile, make the slurry: Mix the flour and 1/2 cup cold water in a cup.
3. When thoroughly mixed, pour the slurry into the boiling water. Stir for 30 seconds, then remove from heat.
4. Put the fruit, lemon juice, and sugar into a blender. Liquefy the fruit while gradually adding the hot water and slurry mixture. When well blended, add the sour cream and combine.
5. Put 1 tablespoon of noodles into each serving bowl, followed by the soup. Garnish with a dollop of sour cream and serve immediately.

White and Red Borschts

White and red are the colors of the Polish flag, and also the colors of two traditional Polish borschts. White borscht is based on pickled bran, and red borscht on pickled beet concentrate; they are not pickled with salt or vinegar. Included here are easy recipes to make your own borscht concentrate.

Pickled Bran for White Borscht:

8 cups water
1/4 pound wheat bran (found in health and organic food stores)
1 small garlic head (about 10 cloves), peeled and sliced
Crust from 1 slice sourdough or pumpernickel bread

1. Boil the water and cool to lukewarm.
2. Put the bran, water, and sliced garlic into a glass or stoneware container. Add the bread crust.
3. Cover with cheesecloth or perforated plastic wrap and secure with a rubber band. Set aside in a warm, dark place for 4 to 5 days.
4. It is ready when it has a pleasant, pungent, and acidic smell. You can use the liquid only, or mix in the bran for a thicker soup. If you do not intend to use it immediately, transfer the liquid to a sealed container and refrigerate; it can be stored in the refrigerator for up to 3 months.

White Borscht garnished with chopped parsley

White Borscht

Serves 6

1 medium onion
1 dried mushroom
1 bay leaf
1 pound smoked meat (ham or kielbasa), cubed
4 cups water
2 medium potatoes, scrubbed
Salt and freshly ground pepper, to taste
1 garlic clove, chopped
1–2 cups liquid from pickled bran, or to taste

Slurry: 1 tablespoon all-purpose flour, 1/2 cup cold water, 2 heaping tablespoons sour cream

1. Put the onion, mushroom, bay leaf, meat, and water into a pot and bring to a boil. Reduce the heat and simmer for 40 minutes.
2. Peel and dice the potatoes.
3. Add salt and pepper to the soup. Add the potatoes and garlic and cook over medium heat until the potatoes are soft. Once the potatoes are done, add the pickled bran liquid (the acidity will prevent the potatoes from cooking if added too soon).
4. Make the slurry and add it to the soup (see page 179). Remove bay leaf. Add salt and pepper.

Pickled Beet Concentrate for Red Borscht:

Tip: Lemon juice will remove beet stains from your hands.

4 cups water
1 pound beets, washed, peeled, and sliced
Crust from 1 slice sourdough or pumpernickel bread

1. Boil the water and cool it to lukewarm.
2. Place the sliced beets in a glass or stoneware container. Pour the prepared water over the beets, and add the bread crust.
3. Cover the container with cheesecloth or perforated plastic wrap and secure with a rubber band. Set aside in a warm, dark place for 4 to 5 days.
4. It is ready to use when it has a pleasant, pungent, and acidic smell. The liquid—not the beet slices—is what you use for borscht (discard the beet slices). If not used for cooking right after pickling, put the liquid into a sealed container and refrigerate for later use. It can be stored in the refrigerator for up to 3 months.

Red Borscht

Serves 6

Red Borscht, served here with Buttermilk Biscuits

This is a recipe for the most popular Polish borscht. Made with pickled beet concentrate, it also calls for stock of any kind—vegetable, chicken, or beef. I find that the tastiest borscht is made with stock from ham bones. Tip: If using store-bought concentrate (simply called "red borscht" on the product label), use 2 cups of stock and 2 cups of concentrate. Red borscht can be served with Mushroom Strudel (page 210) or Little Ear Dumplings (page 150) or sprinkled with Small Puffs (page 206).

2 medium beets, washed, peeled, and sliced
1 dried mushroom
4 cups Homemade Stock (page 178), or stock of your choice
1 tablespoon lemon juice (prevents the soup from losing its red color)
1–2 cups homemade pickled beet concentrate (liquid only)
1 garlic clove, chopped
Salt and freshly ground pepper, to taste

1. In a saucepan over medium heat, cook the beets and mushroom in the stock until soft.
2. Add the lemon juice and pickled beet concentrate little by little, tasting carefully along the way. Adding too much will cause the soup to be too acidic.
3. Add the garlic, and salt and pepper, and cook for a moment longer. Do not cook for too long or the soup will lose its bright color.

Brine Pickle Soup

Serves 6

A strong tradition of pickling exists in Polish cuisine, as evidenced in bread made from a pickled leavening starter, sauerkraut, and pickled herring. Pickling is a process in which food is preserved in a marinade of spices and herbs in either brine or vinegar. For this recipe, do not use pickles pickled in vinegar! Brine pickles can be found in the kosher food section of supermarkets. In some stores, you'll find they are imported from Poland.

6 cups Homemade Stock (page 178), or stock of your choice
3 medium potatoes, scrubbed, peeled, and cubed
5–6 brine (not vinegar) pickles, grated very fine
1 bay leaf
Salt and freshly ground pepper, to taste
Slurry: 2 tablespoons all-purpose flour, 1/2 cup cold water, 2 heaping tablespoons sour cream

1. Pour the stock into a large pot. Add the potatoes and cook over medium heat until the potatoes are soft.
2. Add the grated pickles and the bay leaf to the stock and simmer, covered, for 5 to 10 minutes. Add salt and pepper to taste.
3. Make the slurry (see page 179), stir into the soup, and cook for 1 minute more over medium heat. Remove bay leaf.
4. Serve hot.

Carrot Soup

Serves 4

2 tablespoons unsalted butter
1 small onion, chopped
2 pounds carrots, peeled and diced
2 tablespoons grated fresh ginger
5 bay leaves
2 thin, 3-inch strips of orange zest (without white pith)
1 teaspoon salt, plus more to taste
1/4 teaspoon freshly ground pepper
3 cups Homemade Stock (page 178), or stock of your choice
1 cup orange juice (preferably freshly squeezed)
1/4 cup freshly squeezed lemon juice
1/2 cup heavy cream
Croutons, for serving (optional)

1. Melt the butter in a large pot over medium heat. Add the onion and sauté until golden. Add the carrots, ginger, bay leaves, orange zest, 1 teaspoon of salt, and pepper; simmer, covered, for 5 minutes.
2. Add the stock and cook over low heat until the carrots soften.
3. Remove the bay leaves and orange zest.
4. Allow the soup to cool. Using a blender, puree it thoroughly. Return the soup to the pot.
5. Add the orange and lemon juices and simmer for 5 minutes. Add more salt to taste, if needed.
6. Remove from heat, and stir in the cream. Serve with croutons, if desired.

Cold Summer Soup

Serves 8

A traditional soup in Poland and Lithuania, this soup is refreshing on a hot day and loaded with vitamins.

4 cups Homemade Stock (page 178), or stock of your choice
4–5 small to medium beets (with stems and leaves), washed and finely chopped
Salt and freshly ground pepper, to taste
4 cups buttermilk
2 brine (not vinegar) pickles, chopped
2 cucumbers (use 4 if you do not have the brine pickles), chopped and seeded
1 small bunch scallions, chopped
2 tablespoons chopped fresh flat-leaf parsley
6–10 chopped red radishes (optional)
1 tablespoon chopped fresh dill
8 hardboiled eggs, chopped

Beets give this Cold Summer Soup its pink color.

1. Pour the stock into a large pot; add the beet roots, stems, and leaves and cook over medium heat until the beets are soft. Add salt and pepper to taste. Remove from heat and let cool to room temperature.
2. Add the buttermilk and stir. Add the pickles, cucumber, scallions, parsley, radishes, dill, and more salt to taste (about 1 teaspoon).
3. Cover the soup and chill it in the refrigerator for at least several hours before serving (overnight is best).
4. Serve with 1 chopped egg per bowl.

Potato Soup

Serves 6

This French soup is made in two stages and served with a flavorful little "island" in the center.

2 pounds potatoes, washed and peeled
1 teaspoon salt, plus more to taste
4 tablespoons (1/2 stick) unsalted butter
1/2 teaspoon freshly ground pepper
1 teaspoon ground nutmeg
3 cups Homemade Stock (page 178), or stock of your choice
3 tablespoons vegetable or olive oil
1/2 pound mushrooms, sliced
1 teaspoon chopped fresh flat-leaf parsley, for garnish

Step One:
1. Set 3 potatoes aside for step two. Fill a large pot with water, add the remaining potatoes and 1 teaspoon of salt, and boil until the potatoes are soft.
2. Drain the potatoes, and return them to the pot for 30 seconds over medium heat to steam out excess water.
3. Add the butter, 1/4 teaspoon of pepper, and 1/2 teaspoon of nutmeg, and mash into a puree.
4. Mix the stock into the puree, adding salt to taste.

Step Two:
1. Cube the 3 reserved potatoes. Heat the oil in a skillet over medium heat, and sauté the cubed potatoes until almost soft.
2. Add the mushrooms, the remaining 1/4 teaspoon of pepper, and 1/2 teaspoon of nutmeg. Sauté until tender and the mushrooms release their juices. Add salt to taste.

To Serve:
Pour the mixture from step one into bowls. Spoon 1–1 1/2 tablespoons of the potato-mushroom mixture in the center of each, making a little island. Sprinkle with parsley and serve.

Pumpkin or Squash Soup

Serves 6

6 cups Homemade Stock (page 178), or stock of your choice
2 pounds pumpkin or squash, peeled and roughly chopped
2 medium potatoes, peeled and diced
2 teaspoons minced fresh ginger
1 clove garlic
2 bay leaves
1/2 teaspoon freshly ground pepper
Salt to taste
Soy sauce to taste (optional)
Croutons, for serving (optional)

1. In a large pot, bring the stock to a boil. Add the pumpkin, potatoes, ginger, garlic, bay leaves, pepper, and salt. Lower the heat to medium, and cook until the pumpkin and potatoes soften.
2. Remove from heat, remove bay leaves, and pour the soup into a blender; liquefy. Add salt or soy sauce to taste.
3. If necessary, reheat before serving. Serve with croutons, if desired.

Tomato Soup

Serves 6

A favorite Polish way of serving this soup is with boiled rice.

1 1/2 cup cooked rice or noodles
5 cups Homema de Stock (page 178), or stock of your choice
2–3 tablespoons tomato paste
Slurry: 2 tablespoons all-purpose flour, 1/2 cup cold water,
2 tablespoons sour cream
Salt or soy sauce and freshly ground pepper, to taste

1. In a large pot, bring the stock to a boil. Add the tomato paste and reduce to a simmer.
2. Make and add the slurry (see page 179). Add salt or soy sauce and pepper.
3. Spoon rice or noodles into each bowl, followed by the soup. Serve hot.

Vegetables, Hot and Cold

Every mother says, "Eat your vegetables!" Luckily, we're becoming more and more aware of how important they are in the prevention of many diseases. Even more exciting are the many delicious ways to prepare them. There are a number of salad combinations that are common in Poland, but relatively unknown in the United States, for example, the Celery Root and Apple Salad (page 197). The salads here offer a variety of flavors, from savory Sauerkraut Salad (page 202) to sweet Carrot and Parsnip Salad (page 196).

Belgian Endive, Apple, and Walnut Salad

Serves 4

3 Belgian endives, trimmed
1 large apple, peeled and diced
2 tablespoons raisins
1/2 cup chopped walnuts
1 tablespoon balsamic vinegar
2 tablespoons olive oil
Salt and freshly ground pepper, to taste

Chop the endive leaves into small pieces and mix with the diced apples, raisins, and walnuts. Combine the vinegar, olive oil, and salt and pepper in a separate cup, and pour over the endive mixture.

Cabbage and Apple Salad

Serves 4

1/2 head green cabbage, chopped
2 large sweet apples, diced
1 medium onion, diced
1/4 cup lemon juice
3 tablespoons olive oil
1/2 teaspoon freshly ground pepper
Salt, to taste

Mix all the ingredients together thoroughly.

Carrot and Parsnip Salad

Serves 4

3–4 carrots, peeled and coarsely grated
2 parsnips, peeled and coarsely grated
1 apple, peeled and diced
Salt and freshly ground pepper, to taste
1/2 cup plain yogurt
1/2 teaspoon sugar
1 teaspoon chopped fresh flat-leaf parsley

Mix all the ingredients together thoroughly.

Celery Root and Apple Salad

Serves 4

2 medium celery roots, peeled and coarsely grated
2 medium sweet apples, peeled and coarsely grated
1/2 cup chopped scallions
1 tomato, chopped
Salt and freshly ground pepper, to taste
1/2 cup plain yogurt
1/2 teaspoon sugar

Mix all the ingredients together thoroughly.

Cottage Cheese, Radish, and Scallion Salad

Serves 4

1 pound cottage cheese
1/2 cup chopped scallions or chives
1/2 cup grated radishes
Salt and freshly ground pepper, to taste

Mix all the ingredients together thoroughly.

Egg Salad with Cottage Cheese

Serves 4

3 hard-boiled eggs
1 pound cottage cheese
1/2 cup chopped scallions
Salt and freshly ground pepper, to taste

Peel the eggs and mash them. Mix the eggs thoroughly with the other ingredients.

Mizeria (Cucumber Salad)

Serves 4

I have always wondered why this salad bears such a suggestive name in Polish—I can assure you that it will not make you miserable!

2 large cucumbers, peeled, seeded, and cut into thin slices
1/2 cup plain yogurt
1 teaspoon sugar
Salt, to taste
1/2 teaspoon freshly ground pepper
1/2 teaspoon chopped fresh dill

Mix the cucumbers with the yogurt, then add the sugar, salt, and pepper. Combine thoroughly. Sprinkle the surface with the dill and serve.

Polish Beets Served Warm

Serves 4

Serve this with meats such as brisket, corned beef, or roast beef. It's also good with hamburgers.

3 medium-size beets, washed
1 teaspoon salt, plus more to taste
2–3 teaspoons horseradish or 2 tablespoons lemon juice
2 tablespoons sour cream
Soy sauce, to taste (optional)

1. Place the beets (unpeeled) in a large pot and add just enough water to cover them. Add 1 teaspoon of salt and cook until soft, about 30 minutes. Drain and cool.
2. Peel the beets, grate them finely, and return them to the pot.
3. Stir in the horseradish and sour cream. Add salt or soy sauce to taste and heat over low heat.

Sauerkraut with Mushrooms

Serves 6

3 tablespoons olive or vegetable oil
2 large onions, diced
1 pound mushrooms, chopped (2 cups)
1 pound sauerkraut, drained and finely chopped
1/2 teaspoon salt
1/2 teaspoon freshly ground pepper
2 bay leaves
1/2 pound bacon, chopped
2 tablespoons all-purpose flour

1. Heat the oil in a large skillet over medium heat. Sauté the onions and mushrooms until golden and the juices have been released, about 10 minutes. Add the sauerkraut, and fry together. Add the salt, pepper, and bay leaves. Reduce the heat, cover, and braise for 30 to 40 minutes.
2. Fry the bacon in a separate pan until golden. Add the flour and fry until golden, about 1 minute, stirring constantly.
3. Add the bacon to the sauerkraut and stir. Cook for 1 minute more, stirring. Remove bay leaves.

Tossed Salad with Beets and Sweet Potatoes

Serves 6

2 medium beets, washed
1 1/3 teaspoons salt
2 sweet potatoes, washed and peeled
1 head curly green or romaine lettuce, washed and dried
Yogurt Dressing (page 204) or Vinaigrette (page 203)
1/2 cup pine nuts (optional)

1. Place the unpeeled beets in a pot and cover with water; add 2/3 teaspoon of salt. Bring to a boil and cook until the beets are soft. Drain and cool.
2. Place the potatoes in a pot and cover with water; add the remaining 2/3 teaspoon of salt. Bring to a boil and cook until the potatoes are soft. Drain and cool.
3. Peel the beets and chop them into small cubes.
4. Slice the potatoes into bite-size pieces.
5. Tear the lettuce into bite-size pieces and toss with the cooled beets and potatoes. Toss with the Yogurt Dressing, Vinaigrette, or a dressing of your choice. Sprinkle with pine nuts, if desired.

Tossed Salad with Walnuts, Raisins, and Blue Cheese

Serves 4

Toss this salad with the Vinaigrette on page 203.

1 head lettuce, washed and dried
1/2 cup raisins
1/2 cup walnuts
1/2 cup crumbled blue cheese
Vinaigrette (page 203)

Tear the lettuce leaves into bite-size pieces and add the remaining ingredients. Toss with a vinaigrette dressing.

Tossed Salad with Beets and Sweet Potatoes can be served with Vinaigrette or with Yogurt Dressing, shown here.

Sauerkraut Salad

Serves 4

Never skip oil in salads, as it helps the body absorb vitamins. This salad is particularly high in vitamin C, and you wouldn't want to miss that! This salad is also an excellent accompaniment to Beef Rolades (page 220).

1 pound sauerkraut, drained and chopped
2 tart apples, diced
1 medium onion, diced
2 carrots, peeled and grated
1/2 teaspoon salt, plus more to taste
1/2 teaspoon sugar
1/4 teaspoon freshly ground pepper, plus more to taste
2 tablespoons olive oil

In a large bowl, mix together the sauerkraut, apples, onion, carrots, salt, sugar, and pepper. Add the oil and combine thoroughly. If needed, add more salt and pepper.

Purple-Cabbage-Turned-Pink Salad

Serves 6

This salad complements Polish meat entrées nicely, adding tartness and color. The lemon juice is what turns the cabbage pink.

1 teaspoon salt, plus more to taste
1 medium head purple cabbage, washed and chopped into fine strips
Juice of 1 lemon
2 apples, peeled, cored, and diced
1 medium onion, diced
1 teaspoon chopped fresh flat-leaf parsley
3 tablespoons olive oil
1 teaspoon sugar
Freshly ground pepper, to taste

1. Bring a medium pot of water to a boil. Add 1 teaspoon of salt and the chopped cabbage. Boil until soft, 10 to 15 minutes. Remove the cabbage and drain well.
2. Put the cabbage in a serving bowl and stir in the lemon juice. Set aside to cool completely.
3. Add the apples, onion, parsley, olive oil, and sugar and mix well. Add salt and pepper to taste. Chill, covered, in the refrigerator for 2 hours or overnight.

Vinaigrette

Makes about 1/3 cup

The basic premise is to use 2 parts olive oil to 1 part vinegar and to improvise the remaining ingredients. Whatever you use, it's best to allow the dressing to marinate for at least 30 minutes before use. Here's my suggested version:

3 garlic cloves, minced
2/3 teaspoon salt
3 tablespoons balsamic or red wine vinegar
1 teaspoon mustard of your choice
1 tablespoon chopped fresh basil, or 1 teaspoon dried
1/2 teaspoon freshly ground pepper
1 tablespoon chopped scallions or chives,
1 teaspoon dried oregano
1 tablespoon chopped fresh flat-leaf parsley
6 tablespoons extra-virgin olive oil

1. In a small bowl, mash the garlic and salt together with a fork, making a paste.
2. Add the vinegar, mustard, basil, pepper, scallions, oregano, and parsley and combine. DO NOT add the olive oil until you have thoroughly mixed these ingredients.
3. Add the olive oil and mix thoroughly with a wire whisk or fork.

Yogurt Dressing

Makes about 1 cup

For the best flavor, allow this dressing to marinate for at least 30 minutes before serving. It also makes a great dip for vegetables.

3 garlic cloves, minced
2/3 teaspoon salt
1 cup plain yogurt
1 teaspoon chopped fresh dill
1 teaspoon chopped fresh flat-leaf parsley
1/2 teaspoon freshly ground pepper

In a small bowl, mash the garlic and salt together with a fork, making a paste. Add the remaining ingredients and mix well.

Side Dishes and Appetizers

In Poland, we often have parties where there are no entrées, only a great number of appetizers—in short, lavish cocktail parties. Some of these dishes work best as buffet items, or as light meals in themselves—breakfast, supper, or a snack. Others make good accompaniments to entrées.

Buttermilk Biscuits

Makes 1 dozen

Serve these light, flaky biscuits with soups and appetizers.

2 cups all-purpose flour, plus more for dusting
2 teaspoons baking powder
1/2 teaspoon baking soda
1 teaspoon salt
2 teaspoons chopped fresh herbs (parsley, dill, basil, rosemary, or oregano) or 1 teaspoon spice (paprika or freshly ground pepper) (optional)
1/3 cup vegetable shortening
3/4 cup buttermilk

1. Preheat the oven to 400°. Dust a baking sheet with flour; set aside. Combine the flour, baking powder, baking soda, and salt. If using herbs or spices, mix them in.
2. Using a fork, cut the shortening into the dry ingredients.
3. Mix in the buttermilk with the fork until the dough is consistent and sticky.
4. Use the fork to gently form the dough into a ball, and place it on a surface dusted with flour. The dough must be kept as cool as possible, so avoid using your hands.
5. Roll the dough out to a 1/2-inch thickness. Using a cookie cutter, a drinking glass, or a knife, cut it into 2-inch circles.
6. Place the biscuits on the prepared baking sheet and bake until golden brown, about 20 minutes.

Cheese Biscuits

Makes 2 dozen

An excellent accompaniment to soups, or along with cheese and wine.

10 tablespoons unsalted butter, chilled
8 oz. cream cheese
1/2 teaspoon salt
1 1/4 cups all-purpose flour, plus more for dusting
1 egg, beaten
Poppy seeds, sesame seeds, or herbs, for sprinkling

1. Cut the butter and cheese into small bits. Quickly mix (not thoroughly) the salt, flour, and half of the beaten egg in with the cheese. Form the dough into a ball, wrap it in plastic, and refrigerate for 1 hour.
2. Preheat the oven to 400°. On a lightly floured surface, roll the dough out to a 1/4-inch thickness. Cut it into 1-by-1-inch pieces.
3. Brush the biscuits with the remaining half of the beaten egg and sprinkle with poppy or sesame seeds, or herbs. Bake until golden, 12 to 15 minutes.

Puffs

Makes 1 dozen

Often filled with cream for dessert, puffs can also serve as savory appetizers. You can make small puffs for croutons, or larger ones, as the recipe here will make. Stuff them with cheese, herb butters, or fish pastes. Use a wooden spoon, not a mixer, in this recipe.

8 tablespoons (1 stick) unsalted butter, plus more for the cookie sheet
1 cup hot water
1/2 teaspoon salt
1 cup sifted all-purpose flour
4 eggs

1. Preheat the oven to 450°. Grease a cookie sheet with butter.
2. In a pot, heat the butter, water, and salt until boiling. Throw all of the flour into the butter mixture at once, mixing vigorously with a wooden spoon. Stir until the ingredients form a ball. Remove from heat and allow to cool for 10 to 15 minutes.
3. Add the eggs one at a time, mixing until glossy.
4. Drop the dough, one tablespoon at a time, onto the prepared cookie sheet, 2 inches apart.
5. Bake for 15 minutes, then reduce the heat to 350° and bake for 30 minutes more.

Crêpes

Makes 10 crêpes

Though we think of crêpes as French, they are popular in many European countries, including Poland. We serve them with meat or mushroom fillings as an entrée, or with fruit preserves, whipped cream, or melted chocolate for dessert.

1 cup all-purpose flour
3 eggs
1/2 cup water
1/2 cup milk
2 tablespoons unsalted butter, melted, plus more for frying
Pinch of salt
2 teaspoons sugar (optional; use for sweet crêpes)

1. Mix all the ingredients together well. Cover and refrigerate for at least 30 minutes (refrigerated batter can keep for 2 days).
2. Pour 1 tablespoon of the batter on a hot buttered frying pan and swirl the pan around so that it spreads evenly; fry until golden brown on both sides.
3. To serve, roll up with the sweet or savory filling of your choice.

Fruity Pancakes

Serves 4

Use whatever fruits you have on hand. Try combining three different fruits, for example, apple, peach, and banana. Serve these with maple syrup, honey, or jam.

2 cups buttermilk
3 eggs
2 teaspoons sugar
1/4 teaspoon salt
2 teaspoons baking powder
2 cups whole wheat pastry flour
1 1/2–2 cups chopped fruits or whole berries
Unsalted butter or oil, for frying

1. In a large bowl, mix the buttermilk, eggs, sugar, salt, baking powder, and flour together thoroughly using a wooden spoon or an electric mixer. When the batter is consistent, mix in the fruit.
2. Heat the butter or oil in a skillet and pour about 2 tablespoons of batter per pancake onto the pan. Fry both sides until golden, about 2 minutes per side. Serve hot.

Little Hoof Potato Noodles

Serves 4

These Polish noodles made their way into Italian cooking and, with the addition of cheese, became known as gnocchi (you can make gnocchi from this recipe by adding 2 tablespoons of Parmesan cheese to the dough). Polish or Italian style, these noodles are a perfect accompaniment to braised meats and meats with sauces. They can also be served as an individual dish covered with fried bacon bits.

2 teaspoons salt
2 pounds potatoes, peeled
1 cup all-purpose flour
1 egg

1. Bring a large pot of water to a boil. Add 1 teaspoon of salt and the potatoes, and cook until the potatoes are soft. Drain the potatoes thoroughly and return them to the pot over medium heat to steam away excess water, about 30 seconds.
2. Put another pot of water with the remaining 1 teaspoon of salt over high heat; the noodles must be boiled immediately after being made.
3. Puree the cooled potatoes very thoroughly with a potato ricer or a food processor; there can be no lumps. Mix the flour and egg into the puree.
4. Roll the dough into a cylinder about 1-inch in diameter. Cut diagonally into 1/2-inch noodles (hoof shapes).
5. Throw the noodles into the boiling water immediately. Reduce the heat to medium and stir immediately to prevent them from sticking to the bottom. After the noodles float to the top, cook for 2 minutes, not more. Remove with a slotted spoon.

Middle Eastern Eggplant Dip

Serves 4

1 eggplant
2–3 teaspoons extra-virgin olive oil, plus more for garnish
4 garlic cloves
1/4 cup lemon juice
1 teaspoon salt
1/2 teaspoon freshly ground pepper
2 tablespoons tahini
Olives, for garnish

1. Preheat the oven to 400°. Cut the eggplant in half lengthwise and brush it with olive oil. Bake it until soft, 30 to 40 minutes. Set aside until cool enough to handle.
2. Remove the pulp and discard the skin. Place the pulp in a bowl, cover, and set aside for 1 to 2 hours.
3. Squeeze out excess liquid from the pulp. Put the pulp, garlic, lemon juice, salt, pepper, and tahini in a blender, and mix into a paste.
4. Garnish with olives, pouring a bit of olive oil on top. Serve with vegetable sticks, crackers, toast, or bread.

Mushroom Strudel

Serves 6 to 8

This savory strudel is a traditional complement to soup. It also makes a tasty snack or a light breakfast or supper.

Dough:
2 teaspoons active dry yeast (or 2 ounces fresh)
1/4 cup warm water
1/2 teaspoon sugar
2 cups all-purpose flour, plus more for dusting
2 egg yolks
4–5 tablespoons unsalted butter, melted and cooled to lukewarm
1/2 teaspoon salt
2 tablespoons sour cream
1 egg white, lightly beaten

Filling:
2 tablespoons unsalted butter
1 pound mushrooms, sliced
1 large onion, diced
1 egg
3/4 teaspoon salt
1/2 teaspoon freshly ground pepper

1. Make the dough: Mix the yeast, warm water, and sugar together in a small bowl, and set aside in a warm place until frothy, about 10 minutes.
2. Place the flour in a large bowl and add the yeast mixture, egg yolks, melted butter, salt, and sour cream.
3. Knead well into a fluffy dough, 5 to 10 minutes. It should not stick to your hands; do not add too much flour, however, to avoid tough dough—if the dough is too dry, add more water or sour cream.
4. Cover the dough with plastic wrap and set it aside in a warm place to rise until it doubles in size, 1 1/2 to 2 hours.
5. Meanwhile, make the filling: Melt the butter in a skillet, and fry the mushrooms and onions over medium heat until golden and the juices have been released, 10 to 15 minutes. Let them cool.

6. Grind the mushrooms and onions into a paste with a food processor. Add the egg to the paste and mix. Add the salt and pepper.
7. Now make the strudel: Dust a dry work surface with flour and roll the dough out to a 1/2-inch-thick square.
8. Spread the filling out on the dough, leaving a 1 1/2-inch border free of filling. Starting on one end, roll up the strudel. Tuck the ends under the bottom of the roll.
9. Dust a baking sheet with flour. Place the strudel on the prepared baking sheet. Set it aside, uncovered, in a warm place to rise about 40 percent more, 20 to 30 minutes. Preheat the oven to 400°.
10. Gently brush the strudel with the beaten egg white. Bake until lightly golden, 30 to 40 minutes.

Noodles with Onions and Pepper

Serves 4

During our difficult days in Paris, this humble recipe was often our main course. Luckily, it now appears on my table as a side dish.

1 pound noodles (or rice), cooked according to package directions
3 tablespoons olive or vegetable oil
2 large onions, finely diced
1 teaspoon freshly ground pepper
Salt, to taste

Heat the oil in a large skillet. Fry the onion until golden. Add the pepper and cooked noodles or rice. Mix well, add salt, and serve immediately.

Olive Dip

Serves 4

Serve this dip with toast or Belgian endives or other vegetables.

Olive Dip served with Belgian endives

3 tablespoons olive oil
1 large onion, chopped
3 garlic cloves
1 cup black olives, drained
1/2 cup green olives, drained
1 tablespoon capers, drained
1 tablespoon chopped fresh flat-leaf parsley
1/2 teaspoon freshly ground pepper
1/2 pound feta cheese (optional)

1. Heat the oil in a skillet. Fry the onion until golden.
2. Put the onion, garlic, olives, capers, parsley, pepper, and feta (if using) in a blender or food processor. Grind into a paste that's not too smooth—it should still have some texture.

Oriental Rice

Serves 2

1 cup uncooked rice
4 cups water
1 teaspoon salt
2 tablespoons vegetable or olive oil
2 teaspoons minced garlic
2 teaspoons minced ginger
2 tablespoons chopped scallions
2 tablespoons rice wine vinegar
1 tablespoon sesame oil
1 tablespoon chili oil
1/4 cup soy sauce

1. Boil the rice in the water with the salt and 1 tablespoon of oil until soft. Drain and rinse with cold water. Drain again thoroughly.
2. Heat the remaining 1 tablespoon of oil in a frying pan. Add the garlic, ginger, and scallions and sauté for 30 seconds over high heat, then add the vinegar, sesame oil, chili oil, and soy sauce and stir. Add the rice and mix together over high heat for 1 minute.

Pâté

Makes 24 appetizer servings

An excellent appetizer, pâté is also good in sandwiches. Horseradish complements this very well.

3–4 large dried mushrooms (portobello are best)
1 pound pork loin (with bone)
1 pound stew beef
1 pound chicken thighs with skin
1 pound liver
2 teaspoons salt (or 1 tsp. salt, 1 tsp. soy sauce), plus more to taste
1 teaspoon freshly ground pepper, plus more to taste
3/4 pound lard or chicken skin with fat or bacon fat
1 tablespoon vegetable oil, plus more for pan
2 carrots
1 medium onion
3 garlic cloves
1 parsnip
1 celery rib
2 bay leaves
Bread crumbs, for pan
2 rolls or 5–6 inches French bread
4 eggs
1 teaspoon nutmeg
2 teaspoons marjoram

1. Soak the mushrooms in warm water for 30 minutes before use.
2. Wash all the meat, then sprinkle with 2 teaspoons of salt and 1 teaspoon of pepper.
3. Heat the pork, beef, and chicken thighs with the lard and oil in a large covered pot over high heat. When it bubbles, reduce the heat to a simmer. Add the carrots, onion, garlic, parsnip, celery, and bay leaves.
4. Remove the mushrooms from the water and add to the pot. Simmer, covered, until the meat is soft, about 2 hours. Remove from heat and let cool.

Pâté (front) and Pumpernickel Sourdough Bread (back)

5. Remove any bones. Remove the vegetables and bay leaves. Add the liver and simmer 5 minutes more.

6. Preheat the oven to 350°. Grease a 9-inch round cake pan with vegetable oil and dust it with bread crumbs. Remove the meat and mushrooms and grind them into a smooth paste with a food processor or meat grinder. While grinding the meat, soften the bread in liquid from the pot. When the bread is soaked, add it to the processor, followed by the remaining liquid in the pot.

7. Mix the meat paste, adding salt and pepper to taste.

8. Beat the eggs in a separate bowl together with the nutmeg and marjoram.

9. Mix the egg mixture into the meat paste.

10. Pour the pâté into the prepared pan. Cover completely with aluminum foil. Bake for 1 1/2 hours. Remove and let cool to room temperature.

11. Refrigerate. Do not remove the pâté from the pan until completely chilled. Slice and serve.

Silesian Noodles

Serves 4

*Silesia (*Śląsk*) is a coal-mining region that has both Polish and German traditions. My husband, Jan, was born there. These noodles are a Silesian tradition and, interestingly enough, Silesians call them "Polish noodles." Try serving them with different meats and sauces, or as an individual dish covered with fried bacon bits.*

2 teaspoons salt
6 large potatoes, peeled
1/2 cup potato starch or cornstarch
1/2 cup all-purpose flour
1 egg

1. Fill a large pot with water; add 1 teaspoon of salt and the potatoes. Bring to a boil, reduce the heat to medium, and cook until the potatoes are soft, 20 to 30 minutes.
2. Drain the potatoes thoroughly, and return them to the pot over medium heat to steam away excess water, 30 seconds.
3. Puree the potatoes thoroughly using a potato ricer or food processor; the puree must be very smooth—no lumps! Mix the starch, flour, and egg into the puree.
4. Make the noodles: Form the puree into 1-inch balls. Poke an indentation into each ball.
5. Bring a fresh pot of water with the remaining 1 teaspoon of salt to a boil. Add the noodles to the boiling water. Reduce the heat to medium and stir immediately to prevent the noodles from sticking to the bottom. After they float to the top, cook for 2 minutes, not more. Remove with a slotted spoon, and serve immediately.

Spicy Cold Sesame Noodles

Serves 6

This recipe was given to me by Neil Trager, curator of Jan's 1989 retrospective at the Samuel Dorsky Museum of Art (SUNY New Paltz). Tasty and light, it makes a good buffet table item. It can also be served warm as a side dish.

1 pound fresh egg noodles (or 8 oz. dry linguini)
4 tablespoons sesame oil
1/4 cup light soy sauce
2 tablespoons tahini
1 tablespoon chili oil
1 tablespoon rice vinegar
2 teaspoons minced fresh ginger
2 teaspoons crushed Szechuan peppercorns
2 garlic cloves, crushed in a garlic press

1. Fill a large pot with water and bring to a boil. Add the noodles and 2 tablespoons of sesame oil and cook until al dente.
2. Meanwhile, make the sauce: Combine the remaining ingredients in a separate bowl.
3. Drain the noodles well and immediately mix with the sauce.

Stuffed Eggs

Serves 4

9 eggs
1 roll or 4 inches of a baguette
1/2 cup milk
1 teaspoon chopped dill
2 teaspoons chopped fresh flat-leaf parsley
2 tablespoons unsalted butter, melted, plus 2–3 tablespoons for frying
1 teaspoon salt
1/2 teaspoon freshly ground pepper
2–3 tablespoons bread crumbs

1. Place 8 of the eggs in a pot of water and boil for 10 minutes. Immediately afterwards, place the eggs in ice-cold water for 30 seconds. Remove the eggs and dry them. Do not shell them.
2. Using a sharp knife, gently cut the hard-boiled eggs in half lengthwise. Avoid cracking the shells; they should be as intact as possible.
3. Using a teaspoon, gently remove the eggs from their shells, still being careful not to break or crack the shell. Set the empty shell halves aside.
4. Thoroughly soak the bread in the milk. Squeeze the milk out and place the bread in a bowl or food processor together with the hard-boiled eggs. Mash or process together.
5. Thoroughly mix the dill, parsley, remaining raw egg, 2 tablespoons of melted butter, and the salt and pepper into the mashed eggs.
6. Spoon the mixture into the empty eggshell halves. Fill the shells so that the surface is flat and even, and dip the flat surface into the bread crumbs.
7. Melt 2 to 3 tablespoons of butter in a skillet, and fry the eggs on both sides (shells and all) until golden.

Stuffed Eggs, to be eaten gently with a spoon

Polish Entrées

Situated at the crossroads of Central Europe, Polish cuisine is an amazing mix of ethnic flavors, enriched by French and Italian cooking from the west, Austro-Hungarian cooking from the south, and by Turkish, Tartar, and Mongolian cooking from the east. In large part, the culinary history reflects the political history of Poland. Some Western European influences came from royal marriages, while many eastern influences came in a less delicate fashion, through invasion and war. From all directions came culinary exchange through trade. One of the most famous ancient routes through current-day Poland was the Amber Road, where amber was exchanged for spices such as pepper, cinnamon, nutmeg, paprika, and ginger. For centuries, the region was also a major source of salt and one of the largest suppliers to the rest of Europe. Salt was worth its weight in gold for much of history, so this ingredient, which we now take for granted in cooking, was an important ingredient in Poland's economy.

Beef Rolades

Serves 8

Try serving these with Little Hoof Noodles (page 208) or Silesian Noodles (page 216).

2 pounds beef round
Salt and freshly ground pepper, to taste
2 onions, one sliced, the other diced
1/2 pound bacon, cut into fine strips
1/2 pound sharp cheddar cheese, cut into strips
3–4 pickles, cut into strips
3–4 tablespoons all-purpose flour
Vegetable oil, for frying
1 bay leaf
1 cup beef stock (or 1 bouillon cube dissolved in 1 cup hot water)
2 tablespoons sour cream

1. Cut the beef round into 3/4-inch patties and beat with a tenderizer until 1/2-inch thick.
2. Salt and pepper each patty lightly. In the center of each, place a slice of onion, a strip of bacon, a strip of cheese, and a strip of pickle. Add more pepper.
3. Roll each patty around its filling and close with a toothpick or tie together with thread.
4. Place the flour in a shallow dish. Roll each rolade in flour until it is completely covered with a thin layer.
5. Coat the bottom of a large skillet with oil, and place it over high heat; brown the rolades on all sides.
6. In a separate pot over medium heat, sauté the diced onion in vegetable oil until golden. Reduce the heat to low and add the browned rolades and the bay leaf. Cover and simmer.
7. Using the frying pan in which the rolades were browned, heat the stock until it bubbles. Pour the hot stock into the pot with the rolades and simmer over low heat until tender, about 2 hours. Check occasionally to see if you should add some water. Make sure the rolades don't stick to the bottom of the pot.
8. Remove the rolades from heat, remove the bay leaf, stir in the sour cream, and check the seasoning, adding salt and pepper as necessary.

Beef Rolades with Silesian Noodles (front) and Sauerkraut Salad (back). Also pictured are Jan's three-dimensional box paintings.

Braised Brisket of Beef

Serves 6

Serve with Hoof Noodles (page 208) or Silesian Noodles (page 216), and use the braising liquid as a sauce.

1 beef brisket (about 4 pounds)
3–4 garlic cloves, minced
1 teaspoon salt
1/2 teaspoon freshly ground pepper
2 cups Homemade Stock (page 234), stock of your choice, or 2 bouillon cubes dissolved in 2 cups hot water
2 tablespoons balsamic vinegar or red wine vinegar
1 bay leaf
3 tablespoons all-purpose flour
3 tablespoons olive or vegetable oil
2 tablespoons sour cream

1. Remove the membrane from the brisket and discard.
2. Mash the garlic, salt, and pepper together with a fork, making a paste. Rub the paste into the brisket.
3. Put the brisket in a large container with a cover and pour in 1 cup of stock and the vinegar. Add the bay leaf. Turn the brisket over in the marinade once so that both sides are evenly coated; cover, and refrigerate overnight.
4. Remove the brisket from the marinade and allow excess liquid to drip off. Reserve the marinade. Dust all sides of the brisket with flour thoroughly but lightly.
5. Heat the oil to hot in a skillet. Sear the brisket all over, about 2 minutes per side.
6. Heat the marinade to a boil in a large covered pot. Add the remaining 1 cup of stock to the boiling marinade. Add the brisket and reduce the heat to low. Simmer until tender, about 4 hours.
7. Remove from heat, remove the bay leaf, and stir the sour cream into the braising liquid. Slice and serve.

Chicken in Stock Sauce

Serves 4

This dish is excellent for a delicate stomach. Serve on a bed of white rice.

1 medium onion
1 medium chicken (about 4 pounds)
2 carrots, peeled
2 celery ribs
1 parsnip, peeled
1 teaspoon salt, plus more to taste
1/2 teaspoon freshly ground pepper, plus more to taste
Stock Sauce (page 234)
1 teaspoon chopped fresh flat-leaf parsley, for serving

1. Peel the onion and heat it over an open flame until browned on all sides.
2. Wash the chicken, place it in a large pot, and fill with water until the chicken is half covered. Cook over high heat until boiling, then reduce the heat to low. Skim the foam from the surface and add the carrots, onion, celery, and parsnip. Add 1 teaspoon of salt and 1/2 teaspoon of pepper and simmer until the chicken is tender, 1 1/2 to 2 hours.
3. Remove the pot from heat and cool for 15 minutes before removing the chicken; if you remove it too quickly, it will lose its juices. Cut the chicken into pieces.
4. Using 2 cups of stock from the chicken, follow the recipe for stock sauce on page 234.
5. Place the chicken on a bed of rice, and top with the sauce. Sprinkle with parsley, and add salt and pepper to taste.

Chicken or Veal Cutlets in Dill Sauce

Serves 4

Butter gives these cutlets a delicate flavor. Serve with rice or potatoes.

1 pound chicken or veal cutlets
1/2 teaspoon salt, plus more to taste
2 garlic cloves, minced
1/2 teaspoon freshly ground pepper, plus more to taste
3 tablespoons all-purpose flour
2 tablespoons vegetable or olive oil
2 tablespoons unsalted butter
2 teaspoons chopped fresh dill
2 tablespoons sour cream

1. Using a meat tenderizer, pound the cutlets until 1/2-inch thick.
2. Mash 1/2 teaspoon of salt and garlic together with a fork, making a paste.
3. Rub the paste into both sides of the cutlets and sprinkle with 1/2 teaspoon of pepper. Place the flour in a shallow dish and coat the cutlets lightly on both sides.
4. Heat the oil and butter in a skillet until hot; add the cutlets. Reduce the heat to medium and fry on both sides for about 3 minutes per side (do not try to turn them over too early or they will stick to the skillet).
5. Add the dill. Remove from heat and mix in the sour cream. Add salt and pepper to taste, if needed.

Ground Cutlets (Polish Burgers)

Serves 4

Don't skip the soaked roll—it's the secret behind the most tender ground cutlets your friends have ever tasted! Serve these with french fries or Potato Puree (page 107).

1 dry roll or piece of French bread
1 pound ground turkey (or 1/2 pound pork, 1/2 pound turkey)
1 medium onion, diced
1 egg
1/2 teaspoon freshly ground pepper
1 teaspoon salt or 2 tablespoons soy sauce, or a combination
1/2 cup bread crumbs
3 tablespoons vegetable oil

1. Soak the roll in cold water until soft; remove it and squeeze out excess water.
2. Using a fork or spoon, thoroughly mix the meat, onion, egg, soaked roll, pepper, and salt. Use hands or a spoon to form the mixture into cutlets (about 2 heaping tablespoons per cutlet). Place the bread crumbs in a shallow dish and roll the cutlets to coat.
3. Heat the oil in a skillet over high heat. When the oil is hot, reduce the heat to medium and fry the cutlets, 4 to 5 minutes on each side.

Pierogi

Serves 4

This is one of the most well-known Polish dishes. The method for making the dough is similar to that of the Chinese (scalding the flour) and is perhaps an example of Far Eastern influence. There are a variety of pierogi fillings; included here are two recipes, one sweet and one savory.

Dough:

4 cups all-purpose flour, plus more for dusting
1 teaspoon plus a pinch of salt
1/2 cup boiling water
1/2–1 cup cold water
Filling (recipes follow)
Sour cream, for serving (optional)

1. Pour the flour onto a dry, flat surface (a clean counter will do). Mix in a pinch of salt. Scald the flour by thoroughly mixing in the boiling water with a fork. Mix in the cold water and knead into a soft dough for 4 to 5 minutes. Divide the dough into three parts.
2. On a lightly floured work surface, roll out one portion until 1/8-inch thick—it should be thin, but not enough to tear. Cut into 2 1/2-by-2 1/2-inch squares.
3. Moisten the square edges with water and place 1 teaspoon of filling in the center of each. Fold the squares into triangles around the filling, carefully sealing the edges with a fork. Repeat with the remaining dough.
4. Bring a large pot of water to a boil; add the remaining 1 teaspoon of salt. Add 6 to 8 pierogi, stirring immediately to prevent them from sticking to the bottom. When the pierogi float to the surface, cook for 2 more minutes. Remove using a slotted spoon. Repeat with the remaining pierogi.

Blueberry Filling

Blueberry pierogi are excellent served with a generous dollop of sour cream.

2 pounds fresh blueberries
2 teaspoons sugar
2 teaspoons bread crumbs

Mix the blueberries, sugar, and bread crumbs together thoroughly but gently, making sure to keep the berries whole.

Sauerkraut Filling

The traditional Polish way of serving these pierogi is to garnish them with golden fried onions or onions fried with bacon. An Asian style for serving them is to make a dipping sauce from soy sauce and a bit of vinegar and garlic.

2 pounds sauerkraut
2 tablespoons olive or vegetable oil
1 large onion, diced
1 pound mushrooms, sliced (optional)
Salt and freshly ground pepper, to taste
2 teaspoons cornstarch

1. Drain the sauerkraut well, squeezing it thoroughly. Place it in a pot with just enough water to cover, and bring to a boil. Reduce the heat and simmer, covered, for 30 minutes. Remove from heat and set aside until cool enough to handle.
2. When cooled, drain the sauerkraut well and chop into fine bits.
3. Heat the oil in a skillet and fry the onion (and mushrooms, if using) until lightly golden. (If you're using mushrooms, cook until their juices have been released, 10 to 15 minutes.)
4. Combine the onion mixture with the sauerkraut and add the salt, pepper, and cornstarch. Mix together well.

Meatloaf in front of one of Jan's works

Meatloaf

Serves 6

This can be served warm with potatoes and tossed salad, chilled as an appetizer, or in sandwiches.

Vegetable oil, for pan and loaf
Bread crumbs, for pan
2 dry rolls or pieces of French bread
2 eggs
2 medium onions, diced
2 teaspoons salt
1 teaspoon freshly ground pepper
1 pound ground turkey
1 pound ground pork
3 hard-boiled eggs, shelled

1. Preheat the oven to 350°. Grease a 9-by-4-by-3-inch loaf pan with vegetable oil and dust it with bread crumbs.
2. Soak the rolls in cold water until soft, then remove them and squeeze out excess water.
3. Thoroughly mix the raw eggs, soaked rolls, onions, salt, and pepper into an even mixture. Add the meat and combine.
4. Form the mixture into a loaf around the hard-boiled eggs and place the loaf in the prepared pan.
5. Brush the loaf with vegetable oil. Bake for 1 1/2 to 2 hours.

Pork Loin Chops

Serves 4

Served with Potato Puree (page 107) and Sauerkraut with Mushrooms (page 199), this meal is such a Polish staple that I can't imagine a home where it isn't served!

4 boneless pork loin chops
1/2 teaspoon salt
2 garlic cloves, minced
1/2 teaspoon freshly ground pepper
1 egg
2 tablespoons milk or water
1/2 cup bread crumbs
3 tablespoons vegetable or olive oil
1 tablespoon unsalted butter

1. Using a meat tenderizer, pound the chops until 1/2-inch thick.
2. Mash the salt and garlic together with a fork, making a paste. Rub the paste into each chop on both sides. Sprinkle both sides with pepper.
3. Beat the egg together with the milk. Place the bread crumbs in a shallow dish. Dip each chop in the egg and then in the bread crumbs, making sure that both sides are covered.
4. Heat the oil and butter in a skillet over high heat. Put the chops in the skillet and reduce the heat to medium. Fry each side for about 3 minutes (to avoid sticking, do not turn the chops over until heat has sealed the first side). Do not overcook, as the meat will become tough.

Potato Pancakes

Makes 2 dozen

These can be served with Hungarian Goulash (page 248) or another meat sauce or stew. Some people like them plain, with mustard. Others like them sweet, sprinkled with sugar. Don't get frustrated if the first ones stick and don't come out well—keep the pan hot and well oiled and the next ones should be good. Tip: If you don't have cornstarch or potato starch, you can substitute flour.

3 pounds potatoes, washed and peeled
1 large onion
1 egg
3 tablespoons cornstarch or potato starch
1 teaspoon salt
1/2 teaspoon freshly ground pepper
1 cup vegetable oil for frying, plus more as needed

1. Grate the potatoes finely into a strainer allowing the excess liquid to drip out. Then grate the onion finely.
2. Mix the grated potatoes, onion, egg, starch, salt, and pepper together thoroughly.
3. Heat the oil in a skillet to hot. Spoon 2 tablespoons of the potato mixture into the skillet. Reduce the heat to medium. Fry until golden (about 2 minutes on each side). Do not flip them over until the first side is done and sealed by heat.

Potato ncakes with mushroom sauce (left); ch fruit and gar (center); and with Hungarian Goulash ight). Also ured is one Jan's hand- nted books.

Prune and Apple Sauce for Meats

Serves 6

This sauce is especially complementary to pork, turkey, or chicken.

2 tablespoons olive or vegetable oil
1 large onion, diced
1 cup Homemade Stock (page 234), stock of your choice, or 1 bouillon cube dissolved in 1 cup hot water
12 seedless prunes, finely chopped
2 medium apples, peeled, cored, and diced
2 tablespoons balsamic or red wine vinegar
1 teaspoon sugar
Salt, to taste
2/3 teaspoon freshly ground pepper

1. Heat the oil in a skillet and fry the onion until golden. Add the stock and bring to a boil. Add the prunes, apples, vinegar, sugar, salt, and pepper. Stir, reduce the heat to low, and cover.
2. Simmer for 30 minutes, stirring occasionally to avoid sticking and burning; you can also add a little water if necessary.
3. To serve, spoon about a tablespoon of sauce onto each serving of meat.

Stock Sauce

Serves 4

This sauce is excellent for all kinds of meat. Depending on your preference, you can flavor it with horseradish, mustard, or lemon juice.

1 cup Homemade Stock (page 178), or stock of your choice
2 teaspoons horseradish or mustard, or 1/4 cup lemon juice
Slurry: 2 teaspoons all-purpose flour, 1/2 cup cold water, 2 teaspoons sour cream, 1/2 teaspoon sugar
Salt, to taste

1. Cook the stock and horseradish (or mustard or lemon juice) together in a saucepan for 1 minute over medium heat.
2. In a cup, make the slurry (see page 179). Mix the slurry into the stock mixture. Cook for another 2 minutes over medium heat, stirring constantly. Add salt to taste, if needed.

Little Pigeons (Stuffed Cabbage)

Serves 6

It is probably the shape of the plump and round stuffed leaves that give this dish its name. The Polish name, gołąbki, *means "little pigeons." I find ground turkey or chicken to be the most delicate meat for the stuffing, but you can also use pork. Instead of cabbage leaves you can also use green peppers. Just cut the tops off and clean out the seeds. Fill with stuffing and close with the pepper tops, then continue to follow the recipe. Serve with potatoes or bread. This dish tastes best a day after cooking.*

Stuffing:

3 cups water
2 teaspoons salt
1 tablespoon olive or vegetable oil
1 cup uncooked rice
1 dry roll
1 pound ground meat
1 medium onion, finely diced
1 egg
1/2 teaspoon freshly ground pepper

1. Place the water in a saucepan and add 1 teaspoon of salt and the oil. Bring to a boil and add the rice.
2. Reduce the heat to medium and cook until the rice is soft, about 20 minutes. Drain and rinse with cold water. Set aside to cool.
3. Soak the dry roll in water. When soft, remove and squeeze out excess water.
4. Mix the meat with the onion, egg, 1 teaspoon of salt, pepper, roll, and rice.

Little Pigeons:

1 tablespoon salt, plus more to taste
1 large cabbage head
4 cups Homemade Stock (page 178), or stock of your choice
2 tablespoons tomato paste
Freshly ground pepper, to taste
Slurry: 2 tablespoons all-purpose flour, 1/2 cup cold water, 2 tablespoons sour cream

1. Bring a large pot of water to a boil and add 1 tablespoon of salt.
2. Core the cabbage head about one-third of the way through to remove the stem, and add to pot. Scald the cabbage until the outer leaves are flexible but not soft, about 2 minutes. Reduce heat to simmer.
3. Using tongs, carefully remove the outer leaves of the cabbage, making sure that they remain whole. Repeat until you have 12 to 14 large leaves.
4. Place 1 heaping tablespoon of stuffing in the center of each leaf and fold into a little package. Use a toothpick or thread to close.
5. Bring the stock to a boil in a large pot and add salt to taste. Reduce to a simmer. Using a spoon, delicately lower the "pigeons" into the water. Simmer, covered, for 1 hour.
6. Remove some of the stock, and in a cup, thoroughly mix it with the tomato paste; add pepper. Pour the tomato mixture into the pot.
7. Make the slurry (see page 179) and add it to the pot. Mix and bring to a boil for 1 minute.

Flaki (Tripe Stew)

Serves 6

Don't be afraid to eat tripe—this is a savory and delicious dish!

4–5 pounds beef tripe
4 cups Homemade Stock (page 178), or stock of your choice
1 teaspoon salt, plus more to taste

aki,
companied by
ne of Jan's
and-painted
ooks

2 bay leaves
1/2 teaspoon freshly ground pepper
2 tablespoons unsalted butter (if tripe has no fat)
2 tablespoons all-purpose flour
2 teaspoons dried marjoram
1 teaspoon nutmeg
1 teaspoon paprika
1/2 teaspoon cayenne pepper (optional)

1. Wash the tripe and remove the fat. Set aside 3 tablespoons of fat and discard the rest. Cut the tripe into narrow noodle-like strips.
2. Heat the stock to a boil in a large pot and add the tripe, 1 teaspoon of salt, bay leaves, and pepper. Reduce the heat, cover, and simmer until the tripe is soft, 4 to 5 hours.
3. Make the roux: Chop up the tripe fat and fry it over medium heat. (Use butter if there's not enough fat.) When the fat melts, add the flour; fry until golden, stirring. Remove any remaining pieces of tripe fat.
4. Add the roux to the stewpot. Increase the heat to high and cook for 1 more minute. Add the marjoram, nutmeg, paprika, and, if desired, cayenne pepper. Remove bay leaves and add salt to taste.

Veal Tongue in Horseradish Sauce

Serves 4

Tongue is a very tender cut of meat. It is a delicacy in Poland and Lithuania. Serve this dish with rice or potatoes.

2–3 veal tongues
2 bay leaves
1 teaspoon salt, plus more to taste
1/2 teaspoon freshly ground pepper, plus more to taste
2 teaspoons horseradish
Slurry: 2 teaspoons all-purpose flour, 1/2 cup cold water, 2–3 teaspoons sour cream, 1/2 teaspoon sugar

1. In a large pot, place enough water for the tongues to be covered (don't add the tongues until the water boils; estimate how much water you'll need). Bring to a boil. Add the tongues, bay leaves, 1 teaspoon of salt, and 1/2 teaspoon of pepper. Reduce the heat and simmer until tender, 1 1/2 to 2 hours.
2. Remove the tongues from the pot and, when cool enough to handle, remove the skin (it should come off like a glove) and discard. Cut the tongues into 2-inch slices and return to the simmering broth.
3. Remove 1 1/2 cups broth for the sauce, pour it into another saucepan, and cook over medium heat. Add the horseradish to the broth.
4. Make the slurry (see page 179). Add it to the horseradish sauce and cook for 1 minute more, stirring. Add salt and pepper to taste.
5. Top the tongues with sauce before serving.

Bigos (Hunter's Stew)

Serves 6

This hearty stew is a very traditional winter dish; it is always served on New Year's Eve. Plan ahead when making this: The entire process takes three days.

4–5 dried mushrooms
1 small head cabbage, chopped
1 teaspoon salt, plus more to taste
2 tablespoons vegetable oil
1 large onion, chopped
4 pounds sauerkraut
6 prunes
1 pound fresh chicken bones, pork bones, and/or beef bones, or bones from smoked ham
2 bay leaves
2 pounds of a mix of smoked kielbasa, pork, and smoked ham, chopped into bite-size pieces
Freshly ground pepper to taste
1/2 cup dry red wine (optional)

1. Soak the dried mushrooms in cold water for at least 1 hour.
2. Put the cabbage in a pot and add water until it's just covered. Add 1 teaspoon of salt and bring to a boil. Lower the heat to medium and cook for 20 minutes.
3. Heat the oil in a frying pan and sauté the onion until golden.
4. Rinse and drain the sauerkraut thoroughly with cold water to reduce acidity. Put it in a large pot and add enough water to cover. Remove the mushrooms from the water and add them to the sauerkraut along with the prunes, bones, and bay leaves. Bring to a boil over high heat. Add the cooked cabbage and sautéed onion, then reduce the heat to low and simmer, covered, for at least 6 hours. Cool to room temperature, and refrigerate, covered, overnight.
5. The following day, bring to a boil and stir, reduce the heat to low, and simmer for at least 6 hours. Check occasionally to see if more water is needed. Cool and refrigerate overnight.
6. The next day, bring to a boil, reduce the heat, and simmer for at least 4 hours. Remove the bones.
7. In a skillet, sauté the kielbasa, pork, and ham until golden. Add the meat to the stew and simmer for 30 minutes. Remove bay leaves, and add salt and pepper to taste. Add the wine, if desired, and simmer for an additional 30 minutes before serving.

International Entrées

A wonderful thing about living in America is that one meets people of so many different origins! The following recipes were given to me by such friends. I've taken the liberty of adapting some to my Polish tastes.

Deirdre's Corned Beef

Serves 8

This is our friend Deirdre O'Connor's tasty and surprisingly simple recipe. Irish Americans here serve corned beef with boiled cabbage, potatoes, and carrots. I prefer serving it with a horseradish-flavored Stock Sauce (see page 234), using corned beef broth in place of the stock, along with boiled potatoes and Carrots with Peas, Polish style (recipe follows). In short, a savory Polish-Irish marriage on your plate. Tip: Corned beef broth makes excellent stock for pea, mushroom, or barley soup, so don't throw it out!

1 whole orange
15 whole cloves
4–6 pounds corned beef brisket
2 teaspoons caraway seeds
2 bay leaves
1 teaspoon dried marjoram

1. Wash the orange and stud it with cloves.
2. In a large pot, place enough water to cover the brisket completely, but do not put the brisket into the water yet; just estimate the amount of water needed. Bring the water to a boil. Put the brisket, clove-studded orange, caraway seeds, bay leaves, and marjoram into the pot. Reduce the heat to low and cover. Simmer until the beef is tender, 3 to 4 hours.
3. Cool the brisket in its broth for at least 15 minutes. Remove the brisket just before serving.

Carrots with Peas

Serves 8

2 pounds carrots, peeled and chopped
1 teaspoon salt
2 pounds frozen peas
3 tablespoons butter
2 tablespoons flour

1. Put the carrots in a pot with just enough water to cover them. Add the salt and cook over high heat until carrots are just tender. Add the peas and cook until just tender.
2. In a skillet, heat the butter over medium heat until lightly golden. Add the flour and vigorously stir with a spoon over same heat until evenly golden. Add mixture to the vegetables.
3. Increase the heat and cook until thickened (around 30 seconds), stirring gently all the while. Remove from heat and serve.

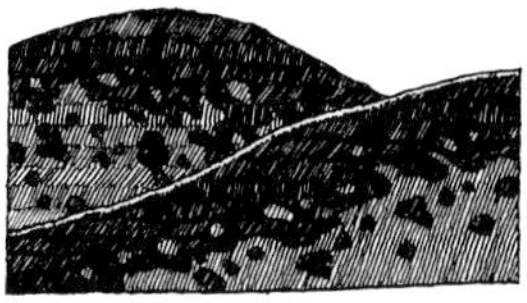

Carmella's Eggplant

Serves 4

This recipe comes from the kitchen of Carmella Corozine, the mother of our painter-writer friend Richard. The Corozine family roots are in Reggio di Calabria, at the very tip of the Italian boot.

1 large firm eggplant, peeled and sliced about 1/2-inch thick
Salt, to taste
Sauce (recipe follows)
1/2 teaspoon freshly ground pepper
3 eggs, lightly beaten
1/2 cup bread crumbs
1/2 cup olive oil
1/2 cup grated Parmesan cheese, plus more for serving

1. Sprinkle the eggplant slices generously with salt. Set them aside for 2 hours to extract bitter juices. Meanwhile, make the sauce.
2. After the sauce is prepared, preheat the oven to 350°. Blot excess moisture from the eggplant slices and sprinkle them with pepper.
3. Put the beaten eggs in a shallow dish and the bread crumbs in another. Heat the oil in a large skillet over medium heat. Dip each eggplant slice into the egg, then into the bread crumbs.
4. Fry until tender and brown, about 1 1/2 minutes per side. Blot each slice with paper towels to remove excess oil.
5. In a baking pan, create alternating layers of sauce, eggplant, and Parmesan cheese (in that order, with sauce on the bottom first). Bake for 30 minutes.
6. Grate more Parmesan cheese on each portion before serving.

Sauce:

2 tablespoons olive oil
1 medium onion, diced
1 garlic clove, minced
One 32-ounce can peeled tomatoes
One 28-ounce can crushed tomatoes
1/2 teaspoon chopped fresh basil or dried basil
1/4 teaspoon fresh or dried oregano

In a medium saucepan, heat the olive oil over medium heat. Sauté the onion and garlic until the onion is transparent. Add the tomatoes, basil, and oregano. Bring to a boil, then reduce the heat to low and simmer for 2 hours (add water as it thickens).

Chicken in Peanut Butter Sauce

Serves 4

In addition to chicken, this sauce can be used with pork, beef, or tofu. You can also add vegetables such as cooked green beans or broccoli. Peanuts or cashews make a great addition, too. Serve with rice.

4 tablespoons (1/2 stick) unsalted butter
1 cup diced onion
2–3 garlic cloves, minced
1–2 teaspoons grated fresh ginger
1 bay leaf
1 tablespoon honey
1 cup pure peanut butter
1/2 teaspoon salt, plus more to taste
2 tablespoons soy sauce
1 tablespoon rice wine vinegar
1/4 teaspoon cayenne pepper
3 cups water
Juice of 1 lemon
1 pound chicken thighs, boned (save bones to make stock!)
Freshly ground black pepper, to taste

1. Make the sauce: Melt 2 tablespoons of butter in a large skillet. Fry the onion, garlic, ginger, and bay leaf until the onion is transparent. Add the honey, peanut butter, 1/2 teaspoon of salt, soy sauce, vinegar, cayenne pepper, water, and lemon juice. Simmer over low heat for 30 minutes, stirring occasionally.
2. Prepare the chicken: Cut the chicken into 1-by-1-inch chunks and sprinkle with salt and pepper lightly.
3. Melt the remaining 2 tablespoons of butter in a separate skillet. Sauté the chicken until golden, 2 to 3 minutes.
4. Add the browned chicken to the sauce and simmer over low heat, 10 to 15 minutes. Remove bay leaf. Salt to taste, if needed.

Chicken with Red Pepper and Yogurt

Serves 4

Tip: Save the thigh bones to make chicken stock. Serve this dish with rice.

1 pound chicken thighs, boned
1/2 teaspoon freshly ground black pepper
3 garlic cloves, minced
1 1/2 teaspoons salt
2 tablespoons olive or vegetable oil
2 tablespoons all-purpose flour
2 large onions, diced
2 tablespoons unsalted butter
2 red bell peppers, seeded and diced
1 teaspoon cinnamon
1/2 teaspoon nutmeg
1/8 teaspoon ground cloves
1/8 teaspoon cayenne pepper
1 teaspoon paprika
2 cups plain yogurt

1. Cut the chicken into 1-by-1-inch chunks. Sprinkle them with black pepper, minced garlic, and 1/2 teaspoon of salt.
2. Heat the oil in a skillet. Place the flour in a shallow dish. Dip each piece of chicken in the flour so it is evenly coated, and sauté until golden, 2 to 3 minutes.
3. In a separate pan, fry the onions in the butter until golden. Add the peppers, cinnamon, nutmeg, cloves, cayenne pepper, and paprika and fry together over high heat for 1 minute. Remove from heat and allow to cool.
4. Put the onions and peppers in a blender. Add the yogurt and the remaining 1 teaspoon of salt and liquefy thoroughly. Return the yogurt mixture to the pan and add the chicken. Cover and simmer over low heat for 30 minutes. Set aside for 15 to 20 minutes to marinate. Reheat before serving, if necessary.

Curried Chicken

Serves 4

Instead of buying ready-made curry, try blending it yourself. Curry is a combination of spices that comes in as many forms as there are tastes. One can make it with just a few spices or a great many. This is my version of basic curry; however, I encourage you to experiment. You can add similar proportions of ground black or green cardamom, cinnamon, ginger, nutmeg, cloves, anise, and saffron. Serve this dish with rice.

Curry:

2 1/2 teaspoons coriander
2 teaspoons cumin
1/2 teaspoon mustard seeds
1/2 teaspoon turmeric
1 teaspoon paprika
1/8 teaspoon cayenne pepper
1/8 teaspoon ground cloves
1 teaspoon salt
1/2 teaspoon freshly ground black pepper

1. Heat the coriander, cumin, and mustard seeds in a frying pan until you smell a strong aroma.
2. In a spice grinder, or with a mortar and pestle, grind them into a powder and combine with the remaining spices.

Chicken:

1 chicken, boned and cut into 1-inch chunks
Curry powder (recipe above)
3--4 tablespoons vegetable oil
2–3 onions, diced
2 teaspoons minced fresh ginger
2 teaspoons minced garlic
1 bay leaf

1 cup tomato sauce
1 bouillon cube dissolved in 1/4 cup hot water
2 cups plain yogurt
Salt, to taste

1. Coat the chicken chunks evenly with the curry. Heat the oil in a large skillet and sauté the chicken until golden, 2 to 3 minutes.
2. Reduce the heat and add the onions, ginger, garlic, bay leaf, tomato sauce, and bouillon water, and braise together for 15 minutes.
3. Remove from heat, remove the bay leaf, and stir in the yogurt. Add salt to taste, if needed.

Eggplant Stuffed with Mushrooms

Serves 4

Tip: Eggplants and mushrooms are vegetables that should never be refrigerated or stored in plastic bags, where they will dampen and spoil; store them in paper bags.

3 tablespoons olive oil, plus more for pan
2 medium eggplants
3 tablespoons unsalted butter
2 medium onions, chopped
1 pound mushrooms, chopped
1/2 cup chopped dried tomatoes
3 garlic cloves, minced
Salt and freshly ground pepper, to taste
1 tablespoon chopped fresh basil, for garnish
Pine nuts or grated Parmesan cheese, for garnish (optional)

1. Preheat the oven to 350°. Grease a baking pan with oil; set aside.
2. Wash the eggplant and cut it in half lengthwise. Grease the cut surface with oil. Place the eggplant halves cut side up on a baking sheet and bake for 30 minutes.
3. When cool enough to handle, spoon out the pulp, leaving a 1/2-inch border of pulp all around the inside.

4. Melt the butter in a large skillet over medium heat. Fry the onions, mushrooms, and dried tomatoes until juices from the mushrooms are released, 10 to 15 minutes. Add the eggplant pulp, garlic, salt, and pepper. Continue to fry until all the ingredients are soft. Remove from heat.
5. Stuff the eggplant shells with the mushroom mixture. Place them on the prepared baking pan and bake for 30 minutes.
6. To serve, sprinkle with basil and, if desired, pine nuts or Parmesan cheese.

Hungarian Goulash

Serves 6

A very popular dish in Poland, goulash was most likely introduced during the Austro-Hungarian partition of southeast Poland in the nineteenth century. At the time, occupied by three nations, the Austro-Hungarians were the most tolerant of Polish language and culture. Perhaps that is why the Poles took an interest in Hungarian cooking! Serve goulash with Potato Pancakes (page 232), Little Hoof Noodles (page 208), or Silesian Noodles (page 216).

2–3 tablespoons olive or vegetable oil
2 medium onions, diced
2 pounds pork round, or boned chicken thighs, cut into 1-inch cubes
Salt and freshly ground pepper, to taste
2–3 tablespoons all-purpose flour
1 cup Homemade Stock (page 178), stock of your choice, or 1 bouillon cube dissolved in 1 cup hot water
2 tablespoons paprika
1 tablespoon tomato paste
2 tablespoons sour cream

1. Heat the oil in a large skillet. Fry the onion until golden and set aside in a medium pot with a cover.
2. Sprinkle the meat lightly with salt and pepper. Place the flour in a shallow dish and thoroughly coat the meat with a thin layer of flour.
3. Heat the skillet over high heat, and sear the meat on all sides, adding more oil if necessary. Add the meat to the onions in the pot.
4. Heat the stock to a boil in the skillet in which the meat was fried, scraping up any browned bits that are stuck to the pan. Add the stock and paprika to the pot. Cover and simmer over low heat until the meat softens, about 2 hours.
5. Before serving, mix in the tomato paste and sour cream. Add salt to taste.

Korean-Style Chicken

Serves 4

Serve with Oriental Rice (page 213) and grilled vegetables.

Marinade:

2 tablespoons rice wine vinegar
3 tablespoons soy sauce
3 garlic cloves, minced

1 pound boneless, skinless chicken breasts
3 tablespoons olive or vegetable oil

Sauce:

Juice of 2 limes or lemons
2 garlic cloves, minced
2 tablespoons soy sauce
1/2 teaspoon grated lime or lemon zest
2 teaspoons water

1. Make the marinade: Mix the ingredients together and place in a resealable plastic bag or container. Soak the chicken in the marinade for at least 30 minutes (overnight is best) in the refrigerator.
2. Preheat a grill or grill pan. Remove the chicken from the marinade and discard the marinade. Brush the chicken with oil and cook on the grill for no more than 10 minutes, taking care that both sides are evenly cooked. Remove the chicken from the grill and set aside for 5 minutes to rest.
3. Make the sauce: Thoroughly mix the ingredients.
4. To serve, cut the chicken into pieces and top with sauce.

Sautéed Chicken in Buttermilk Marinade

Serves 2

Serve this dish with rice.

1/2 cup buttermilk
1/2 teaspoon freshly ground pepper
1 teaspoon salt
2 teaspoons minced fresh garlic
2 teaspoons paprika
1 pound boneless, skinless chicken breasts
1/2 cup all-purpose flour
2 tablespoons olive or vegetable oil

1. Make the marinade: Combine the buttermilk, pepper, salt, garlic, and paprika in a resealable plastic bag or container. Soak the chicken in the marinade for at least 30 minutes (overnight is best) in the refrigerator.
2. Place the flour in a shallow dish. Heat the oil in a large skillet. Remove the chicken from the marinade, letting the excess liquid drip off. Discard the marinade. Dip the chicken in the flour, coating both sides, and place it in the hot skillet. Fry each side for 3 to 4 minutes.
3. Remove the chicken from the frying pan and allow it to rest a moment before serving.

Chicken Mole

Serves 4

This is adapted from my friend Graciella's recipe. She comes from Cuernavaca, Mexico, and now lives in the United States. As do her family's roots, the origins of this dish lie in the glorious past of the pre-Columbian Indian civilizations of Mexico. In those times, however, chocolate was used primarily in a ritual drink called "water of the gods," reserved for upper class men. What an injustice, when it is women who seem to love chocolate the most!

Although it's not quite the same, you can replace the chiles with 1/2 to 1 teaspoon of cayenne pepper, 1/2 teaspoon of flaked cayenne pepper, and 1 tablespoon of paprika. Serve this dish with rice, and save leftovers for the Chicken Burritos recipe (page 254).

2 oz. (about 4) dried ancho chiles
1 oz. (about 2) dried mulato chiles
1/3 oz. (about 1) dried pasilla chile
1/3 cup olive or vegetable oil
1/2 cup raisins
2 tablespoons sesame seeds, plus more for garnish
1 medium onion, chopped
2 garlic cloves, chopped
1 slice stale bread
1 oz. (2 heaping tablespoons) shelled peanuts or almonds, or peanut butter
2 ripe tomatoes, roasted, peeled and chopped, or 2 teaspoons tomato paste
1/2–1 teaspoon anise seeds (optional)
1 oz. bitter dark chocolate or 1/4 tablet Mexican chocolate, grated or 2 teaspoons cocoa powder
1 1/2 cups Homemade Stock (page 178), or stock of your choice
1/2 teaspoon freshly ground pepper, plus more for the chicken
1/8 teaspoon ground cloves
1 teaspoon cinnamon
1 bay leaf
1 medium chicken, quartered
1 teaspoon salt

1. Slice the chiles in half lengthwise and remove the seeds and veins; reserve 2 tablespoons of seeds and discard the rest.
2. Place a pot of water over high heat and bring to a boil. Heat 2 tablespoons of the oil in a skillet and fry the chiles briefly, just until they release their aroma. Drop the chiles into the boiling water and cook until softened; remove and set aside.
3. Boil the raisins in the water for 1 minute and drain; put them in a blender.
4. Fry 2 tablespoons of sesame seeds and the reserved chile seeds in the skillet until golden; add to the blender.
5. Sauté the onions in 2 tablespoons of oil with the garlic until the onions are transparent, then add them to the blender.
6. Soak the bread in water until soft; squeeze out excess water, and add it to the blender.
7. Put the chiles, peanuts, tomatoes, anise seeds (if using), grated chocolate, and stock in the blender. Liquefy all the ingredients thoroughly. Pour this mixture into a saucepan and stir in the 1/2 teaspoon of pepper, the cloves, cinnamon, and bay leaf. Simmer over low heat.
8. Sprinkle the chicken lightly with salt and pepper. Fry it in the remaining 2 teaspoons of oil over high heat for 5 minutes, then over medium heat until golden on both sides and cooked through.
9. Add the chicken to the sauce and simmer for a minimum of 10 minutes before serving, or remove from heat and refrigerate overnight, not removing the chicken from the sauce, and reheating before serving.
10. To serve, remove the bay leaf and sprinkle with sesame seeds.

Chicken Mole is served with rice (left) and corn tortillas (right).

Chicken Burritos

Serves 8

This is a great way to use leftover mole sauce and chicken. Make a fresh batch of rice to serve on the side.

1–2 cups mole sauce
4 cups shredded leftover chicken
8 tortillas
2 cups diced red onions
1 pound mozzarella cheese, grated

1. Preheat the oven to 400°. Heat up the mole sauce in a pot set over low heat. Heat the chicken in a microwave.
2. Place the tortillas on baking sheets and bake just enough to soften, 2 to 3 minutes—do not overbake, or they will harden!
3. Remove the tortillas from the oven and place 1/2 cup of chicken, 1 tablespoon of onion, and 1 tablespoon of grated mozzarella on each tortilla and roll up.
4. Top the burritos with warm mole sauce and serve.

Spanish Chicken

Serves 4

Serve this chicken with white rice.

1 medium chicken (3–4 pounds)
1/2–3/4 teaspoon salt, plus more to taste
2 tablespoons vegetable oil
1 large onion, diced
1 (12–14 ounce) can pitted black olives
6 anchovy fillets
1 teaspoon capers
1/2 teaspoon freshly ground pepper
1/2 cup dry white wine
1 teaspoon mustard (any kind)
1 teaspoon chopped fresh flat-leaf parsley, for garnish (optional)

1. Wash and quarter the chicken, and salt it lightly. Heat the oil in a large pot over high heat and sear the chicken.
2. Reduce the heat to low, add the onion, and stir.
3. Process, grind, or chop the olives into fine bits and add them to the pot.
4. Add the anchovies, capers, and pepper and stir. Add the wine and mustard. Stir, cover, and simmer for 20 to 30 minutes. Add salt to taste.
5. Sprinkle with parsley and serve with rice.

These are a collection of my favorite dessert recipes. Some are typically Polish, while others come from friends at home and abroad. Tip: Butter should not be substituted with margarine or other fats, as nothing can replace its flavor. Do not use salted butter in these recipes, or you will end up with a salty dessert.

Apple Spice Cake

Makes one 7-by-12-inch or 8-by-8-inch cake

This light, moist cake is perfect for any occasion.

Unsalted butter, for pan
Bread crumbs, for pan
1 cup raisins
1/3 cup vegetable oil
1 cup sugar
Pinch of salt
1 egg
1 cup all-purpose flour
1 teaspoon baking soda
1/2 teaspoon nutmeg
1 teaspoon pure vanilla extract
2 teaspoons cinnamon
2 cups chopped apples
1/2 cup chopped walnuts

1. Preheat the oven to 350°. Butter a 7-by-12-inch or 8-by-8-inch baking pan and dust with bread crumbs.
2. Put the raisins into a small pot and add just enough water to cover them. Bring to a boil and remove from heat. Drain the raisins, reserving the water; set aside.
3. In a large bowl, cream together the oil, sugar, and salt, using a wooden spoon. Add the egg and mix. Add the flour, baking soda, nutmeg, vanilla,

and cinnamon; mix thoroughly. Fold in the apples, nuts, raisins, and 2 tablespoons of the reserved water.

4. Pour the mixture into the prepared pan and bake until lightly browned on top, about 40 minutes.

5. Let it cool for 10 minutes in the pan, then cut into 2-by-2-inch squares for serving.

100-Year-Old Fruity Cake

Makes one 10-inch cake

This recipe is from a very old lady neighbor in Upstate New York, and it is surely around 100 years old. You can use whatever fruit is in season—plums, peaches, pears, blueberries, apples, or others. Larger fruits (peaches and apples) should be quartered, plums halved, and small fruits (berries) should be used whole.

Cake topping:

1 1/2–2 cups fruit (enough to completely cover the batter)
1 teaspoon lemon juice
1 teaspoon cinnamon
1 teaspoon sugar

Cake:

8 tablespoons (1 stick) unsalted butter, at room temperature, plus more for pan
Bread crumbs, for pan
3/4 cup sugar
2 eggs
1 teaspoon baking powder
Pinch of salt
1 teaspoon grated lemon or orange zest
1 teaspoon pure vanilla extract
1 cup all-purpose flour

1. Preheat the oven to 350°. Butter a 10-inch springform pan and coat with bread crumbs.
2. Make the topping: Mix the fruit with the lemon juice, cinnamon, and sugar; set aside.
3. Make the cake: Beat the butter and sugar together in a large bowl. Add the eggs, and beat. Add the baking powder, salt, zest, and vanilla; mix thoroughly. Add the flour; mix thoroughly.
4. Pour the batter into the prepared pan. Top with the fruit mixture and lightly press into the batter.
5. Bake for 60 minutes. Let the cake cool for 10 minutes before removing it from the pan. Cool completely before serving.

Cheesecake Mousse

Serves 6

This can be made in a graham cracker crust or as individual servings.

2 sheets or 1 sachet gelatin
2 tablespoons warm water
1 cup fruit, plus additional fruit for decorating
8 oz. cream cheese
2 tablespoons sugar
2 tablespoons lemon juice
Ready-made graham cracker crust (or use recipe on page 260)

1. Dissolve the gelatin in the warm water.
2. Liquefy 1 cup of fruit in a blender.
3. In a bowl, cream the cheese with the sugar. Add the liquefied fruit and mix. Add the lemon juice and gelatin. Mix well.
4. Pour the filling into the graham cracker crust or individual bowls, and refrigerate for 2 hours or until set. Decorate with the remaining fresh fruit before serving.

Variation:

Fruit-flavored instant Jell-O can replace fresh fruit.

1 cup water
3 oz. fruit-flavored instant Jell-O
8 oz. cream cheese
Graham cracker crust

1. Put the water in a pot over high heat to boil. When it boils, dissolve the instant Jell-O in the water. Reduce the heat and simmer for 2 minutes or until fully dissolved. Remove from heat and cool slightly.
2. Add the cream cheese and mix thoroughly.
3. Pour the filling into the graham cracker crust or individual bowls, and refrigerate until set.

Clockwise from left: 0-Year-Old Fruity Cake made with plums; Cheesecake Mousse; and Cheesecake garnished th preserves made from rries grown our garden

Cheesecake

Makes one 10-inch cheesecake

Graham cracker crust:

6 tablespoons (3/4 stick) unsalted butter, melted
1 1/4 cups graham cracker crumbs (16 graham crackers)
2 tablespoons sugar

Filling:

5 eggs, separated
3/4 cup sugar
1 tablespoon pure vanilla extract
1 teaspoon grated lemon zest
3/4 cup sour cream
2 cups cottage cheese
2 tablespoons all-purpose flour
Cherry preserves (optional)

1. Make the crust: Preheat the oven to 325°. Mix the butter, crumbs, and sugar together in a bowl. Press the mixture into the sides and bottom of a 10-inch springform pan. Bake for 15 minutes. Remove and let cool.
2. Make the filling: With a handheld mixer, beat the egg whites and 2 tablespoons of the sugar until stiff.
3. In a separate bowl, beat the egg yolks and the remaining sugar until thick. Mix in the vanilla and lemon zest. Gradually add the sour cream and cottage cheese, beating thoroughly until creamy. Mix in the flour.
4. Fold the beaten egg whites into the cheese mixture.
5. Pour the filling into the cool crust. Bake the cake for 90 minutes. To prevent the top from cracking, place a pan of water on the rack below the cake.
6. After removing the cake from the oven, immediately run a knife between the cake and the pan—this also prevents cracks. Serve chilled, and top with cherry preserves, if desired.

Cranberry Scones

Makes 12 scones

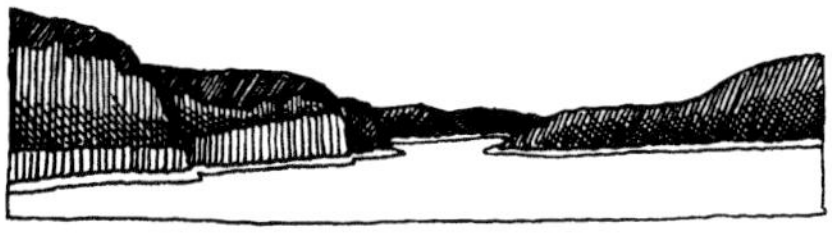

Scones are popular at breakfast or tea time in Britain, where they're served warm with clotted cream and fruit preserves. As an alternative to cranberries, try this recipe with blueberries or chopped fruit—peaches, apricots, or pears.

2 cups all-purpose flour, plus more for dusting
1 teaspoon baking powder
6 tablespoons (3/4 stick) cold unsalted butter
2 eggs
1 tablespoon sugar, plus more for sprinkling
Pinch of salt
1/3 cup sour cream
2 teaspoons pure vanilla extract
1 teaspoon grated lemon or orange zest
1 cup fresh or frozen cranberries
Beaten egg or sour cream, for glazing

1. Preheat the oven to 400°. Dust a baking sheet with flour. Mix the flour and baking powder together in a bowl. Using a fork, cut the butter into the flour mixture until only pea-size chunks remain.
2. Add the eggs, sugar, salt, sour cream, vanilla, and zest and gently mix, still using the fork. (Do not use your hands, as the dough must be as cool as possible). Mix in the cranberries.
3. Form the dough into a ball. On a lightly floured surface, roll it to a 3/4-inch-thick circle (use as little flour as possible). Cut into twelve 2 1/2-inch-long triangles.
4. Place the scones on the prepared baking sheet. Glaze with the beaten egg or sour cream, and sprinkle some sugar on top. Bake until golden brown, about 20 minutes.

Edith's Strudel

Makes 4 dozen pieces

This dessert is a favorite of photographer Andrea Barrist Stern's mother. It comes from the Jewish tradition.

1/2 cup (1 stick) unsalted butter
1/2 cup cream cheese
2 cups all-purpose flour, plus more for dusting
Sugar and cinnamon, for sprinkling
1 pound walnuts, chopped
1 1/4 pounds golden raisins
1 1/4 cups strawberry preserves, or preserves of your choice (fig or date preserves add a Middle Eastern flavor)
1/4 cup sour cream, for glazing

1. Using an electric mixer, cream together the butter and cream cheese. Cut in the flour with a pastry blender or two knives; knead together well.
2. Divide the dough into 4 portions. Make a ball out of each, wrap in plastic, and refrigerate for 1 hour.
3. Preheat the oven to 400°. Line 2 baking sheets with aluminum foil and dust with flour. On a board dusted with flour roll one ball of dough into a 1/8-inch-thick oval, about 8 by 12 inches. Sprinkle with sugar and cinnamon. Sprinkle with a quarter of the walnuts and raisins. Drop about 14 teaspoons of preserves evenly over the walnuts and raisins.
4. Starting from one of the longer sides, roll the dough into a log. Seal the roll by folding the outer edge in on itself, and further secure it by folding and tucking the ends under the bottom (to prevent the preserves from spilling out during baking). Transfer the log carefully onto a prepared cookie sheet. Repeat steps 3 and 4 with the remaining dough.
5. Spread 1 tablespoon of sour cream on each roll and bake until golden, about 20 minutes.
6. Cool completely, then cut each log into 12 pieces.

Fresh Fruit Compote

Serves 6

A light dessert, this is delicious and refreshing on a hot summer day.

1 pound fruit of your choice (apples, pears, strawberries, or other)
4 cups water
2 tablespoons sugar
1/4 teaspoon cinnamon
1/4 teaspoon ground cloves
Juice of 1 lemon

1. Peel, core, and chop the fruit.
2. In a large pot, bring the water and sugar to a boil. Add the fruit, cinnamon, cloves, and lemon juice. Reduce the heat to medium and cook for 3 to 5 minutes.
3. Serve at room temperature or chilled.

Greek Butter Cookies

Makes about 40 cookies

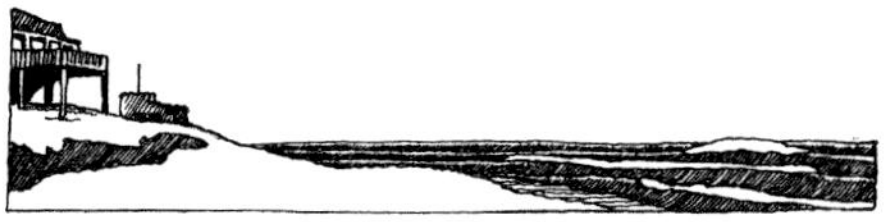

This recipe was given to me by Greek friends whom we met during our first American summer vacation in Asbury Park, New Jersey.

1 cup (2 sticks) unsalted butter, softened
1/4 cup vegetable oil
1 cup sugar
4 large eggs
2 teaspoons pure vanilla extract
1/4 cup fresh squeezed orange juice
1 teaspoon grated orange zest
3 teaspoons baking powder
2 tablespoons milk
4 1/2–5 cups all-purpose flour

1. In a large bowl, beat the butter and oil together until creamy. Add the sugar and beat. Add 3 eggs, one at a time, beating well. Beat in the vanilla, orange juice, orange zest, baking powder, and milk. Beat in the flour; the dough should be soft. Cover the bowl with plastic wrap and chill for at least 2 hours, or overnight.
2. Preheat the oven to 350°. Dust two baking sheets with flour. Remove about 1 tablespoon of dough and roll it into a 6-inch-long, 1/2-inch-thick cylinder. Fold the cylinder in half and twist the two halves together. Place the cookie on a prepared baking sheet. Repeat with the remaining dough.
3. Beat the remaining egg in a bowl and brush it lightly on the cookies. Bake until golden, about 20 minutes.
4. Remove the cookies from the baking sheets as soon as they are just cool enough to touch or they will stick. Cool completely on a wire rack or directly on a serving dish.

Faworki (Kindling Cookies)

Serves 10

These are consumed in great amounts in Poland during the winter carnival and on Fat Thursday, the day before the Lenten fast begins. The alcohol prevents the dough from absorbing too much fat, keeping the cookies light and delicate.

2 pounds vegetable shortening
3 cups all-purpose flour, plus more for dusting
6 egg yolks
3 1/2 tablespoons sour cream
2 teaspoons baking powder
2 teaspoons pure vanilla extract
1/2 teaspoon salt
1 tablespoon vodka
Confectioners' sugar, for sprinkling

1. In a deep skillet, heat the shortening to 375°.
2. In a large bowl, thoroughly mix the flour together with the yolks, sour cream, baking powder, vanilla, salt, and vodka; the dough must be soft.
3. Divide the dough into 2 or 3 portions. On a very lightly floured surface, roll out the dough as thinly as possible. Cut the dough into 1-by-5-inch strips. About 1 inch from each strip's end, cut a slit down the center that ends about 1 inch before the other end. Fold one end of the strip through the slit and gently pull it through.
4. Deep-fry the cookies in the shortening until golden.
5. After frying, place the cookies on paper towels to absorb excess oil, and sprinkle generously with confectioners' sugar.

Clockwise from left: Kindling Cookies with Crescent Cookies; Fresh Fruit Compote; and Strawberry Mousse. Jan's painting is in the background.

Meringue Torte

Makes one 10-inch torte

My guests die for this! It consists of layers of meringue and rich and dreamy icing.

Unsalted butter, for pans
1 cup egg whites (about 8 large whites)
1 teaspoon lemon juice or vinegar
2 teaspoons pure vanilla extract
2 cups plus 2 tablespoons sugar
Icing (recipe follows)
Flaked dried coconut, for sprinkling (optional)

1. Preheat the oven to 250°. Grease three 10-inch springform pans with butter.
2. Place a few inches of water in the bottom of a double boiler and put over high heat. In the top pot of the double boiler (not over heat) start beating the egg whites, lemon juice, vanilla, and 1/4 cup of the sugar. When soft peaks form, put the top pot over the boiling water and continue beating, gradually adding the remaining sugar. Beat over heat until the mixture is quite stiff, about 15 minutes. Remove from heat.
3. Divide the mixture equally among the prepared pans, spreading evenly with a rubber spatula. You can also use a baking sheet, being careful to spread the batter into 3 equal circles (cut out circles of waxed paper, spread vegetablé oil or butter on the surface, sprinkle lightly with flour, and then spread the batter on them).
4. Bake for 3 hours. When done, turn the oven off and let the meringues cool and dry inside. While the meringues are still quite warm, gently nudge them off the pans; leave them in the oven to cool and dry completely.
5. Place one meringue on a serving platter and spread with icing. Top with another meringue, followed by icing, and repeat with the third layer. Smooth icing on the sides first, then the top. If desired, sprinkle with coconut. Chill for a minimum of 2 hours before serving.

Meringue Tort decorated with coconut flakes and fresh flowers

Icing:

One 14-ounce can sweetened condensed milk
2 tablespoons instant coffee dissolved in 1 tablespoon hot water
2 teaspoons pure vanilla extract
1 pound (4 sticks) unsalted butter, at room temperature

1. Combine the condensed milk with the dissolved coffee and vanilla.
2. In a separate bowl, beat the butter.
3. The condensed milk mixture and the butter mixture must be at the same temperature in order to combine. Slowly add the butter mixture to the condensed milk mixture, beating continuously. If the ingredients do not combine, refrigerate both until the temperatures are equal and try again.

Orange Cake

Makes one 10-inch cake

Tip: Wash the orange with baking soda to remove any pesticides.

1/2 cup (1 stick) unsalted butter, melted, plus more for pan
Bread crumbs, for pan
1 medium–large orange, washed
2 large eggs
1 1/4 cups sugar
Pinch of salt
2 teaspoons pure vanilla extract
2 teaspoons baking soda
1 teaspoon baking powder
1/4 cup orange juice or buttermilk
1 1/2 cups all-purpose flour
1 cup chopped walnuts
Confectioners' sugar or warmed fruit preserves, for serving (optional)

Orange Cake, garnished with my homemade preserves

1. Preheat the oven to 350°. Grease a 10-inch cake pan with butter and dust with bread crumbs.
2. Leaving the peels on, chop the orange, seed it, and liquefy in a blender.
3. In a large bowl, combine the eggs, sugar, salt, vanilla, baking soda, and baking powder. Add the orange, melted butter, and orange juice or buttermilk. Gradually beat in the flour. When the mixture is consistent, fold in the nuts.
4. Pour the batter into the prepared pan. Bake until a knife inserted into the center comes out clean, 50 to 55 minutes.
5. Cool for 10 minutes before removing the cake from the pan. To serve, sprinkle with confectioners' sugar or glaze with warmed fruit preserves, if desired.

Rhubarb Crisp

Serves 8

1/3 cup unsalted butter, plus more for dish
4 cups chopped rhubarb
1/2 teaspoon salt
1 1/3–2 cups sugar
3/4 cups all-purpose flour
1 teaspoon cinnamon
Whipped cream or vanilla ice cream, for serving (optional)

1. Preheat the oven to 350°. Grease a 10-by-6-by-2-inch baking dish with butter. Place the rhubarb in the prepared baking dish and sprinkle with salt.
2. Mix the sugar, flour, and cinnamon in a separate bowl. Cut in the butter until the mixture resembles coarse crumbs. Sprinkle evenly over the rhubarb.
3. Bake for 40 to 50 minutes.
4. Serve warm with whipped cream or vanilla ice cream, if desired.

Strawberry Mousse

Serves 4

Replace strawberries with raspberries for another delightful mousse.

1 tablespoon powdered gelatin (or two sheets)
1/3 cup hot water
1 cup strawberries, washed and hulled
2 egg whites
1/2 cup confectioners' sugar
1 teaspoon pure vanilla extract
1 tablespoon lemon juice
1/2 cup whipping cream

1. In a small bowl, melt the gelatin in the hot water and set aside to cool completely.
2. Set aside a few strawberries for decorating, and liquefy the rest in a blender or food processor.
3. In a large bowl, beat the egg whites with 1/4 cup of confectioners' sugar until soft peaks form. Add the vanilla, lemon juice, and cooled gelatin.
4. In a separate bowl, beat the cream with the remaining 1/4 cup of confectioners' sugar until soft peaks form. Set a little of the whipped cream aside for decorating.
5. Gently fold the strawberry mixture and the whipped cream into the egg white mixture. Pour into individual bowls and chill for 2 hours or overnight (overnight is best).
6. To serve, decorate with the reserved strawberries and whipped cream.

Tiramisu

Makes one 8-by-8-inch dessert

6 oz. semisweet chocolate chips
1 tablespoon unsalted butter
1 cup heavy cream
4 eggs, separated
3 teaspoons sugar
2 teaspoons pure vanilla extract
20 ladyfingers
1 cup strongly brewed coffee
1/4 cup brandy or sweet wine
Shaved chocolate or cocoa, for garnish

1. In a double boiler, melt the chocolate chips. Add the butter and 1/4 cup of heavy cream and mix. When the chocolate and butter have melted, remove from heat. Fold in the egg yolks.
2. In a separate bowl, use an electric mixer to beat the egg whites with 1/2 teaspoon of sugar until soft peaks form.
3. Fold the egg whites into the chocolate mixture.
4. In another bowl, whip the remaining 3/4 cup of heavy cream with the remaining 2 1/2 teaspoons of sugar and the vanilla.
5. Mix the coffee with the brandy or sweet wine. Using half of the ladyfingers, quickly dip each cookie in the coffee mixture and use them to line the bottom of a 8-by-8-inch serving dish.
6. Spread half of the chocolate mixture onto the layer of moistened ladyfingers.
7. Spread half of the whipped cream over the chocolate.
8. Dip the remaining ladyfingers in the coffee mixture and use them to create another layer. Follow with another layer of chocolate, and then whipped cream.
9. Sprinkle the top with chocolate shavings or cocoa. Refrigerate overnight before serving.

Walnut Torte

Makes one 10-inch torte

Cake:

Unsalted butter, for pan
3 tablespoons bread crumbs, plus more for pan
8 eggs, separated
2 cups confectioners' sugar
1/4 cup lemon juice
2 teaspoons pure vanilla extract
2 cups walnuts, ground

Soaking Mixture:

Juice of 1/2 lemon
1/4 cup liquor of your choice (Cointreau or rum are excellent)
1/4 cup water

Frosting (recipe follows)

1. Preheat the oven to 350°. Grease a 10-inch round baking pan with butter and dust it with bread crumbs.
2. Make the cake: In a large bowl, use an electric mixer to beat the egg whites with 2 tablespoons of confectioners' sugar and 1 tablespoon of lemon juice until soft peaks form.
3. In a separate bowl, beat the yolks with the remaining sugar, lemon juice, and vanilla until fluffy. Add the ground walnuts and the bread crumbs, and mix well.
4. Gently fold the egg whites into the yolk mixture.
5. Gently transfer the batter to the prepared baking pan. Bake until golden brown, about 40 minutes.
6. Turn off the oven, and leave the cake inside to cool. When completely cool, remove from pan.
7. Meanwhile, make the soaking mixture: Combine the lemon juice, liquor, and water.

8. With a long, serrated knife, carefully cut the cake horizontally into 2 or 3 layers.
9. Place the bottom layer on a serving dish. Gently spoon half (if 2 layers of cake) or one-third (if 3 layers of cake) of the soaking mixture over this layer. Spread the cocoa (or lemon) frosting on top. Place the second layer of cake on top of the first and add soaking mixture. Spread with lemon (or cocoa) frosting. Repeat with the third layer, if using.

Frosting:

1 1/2 cups sugar
4 whole eggs
2 egg yolks
1 tablespoon pure vanilla extract
1 pound (4 sticks) unsalted butter, at room temperature
1 tablespoon liquor of your choice
2 tablespoons cocoa
Juice of 1 lemon

1. In the top of a double boiler with the water on simmer, beat the sugar, whole eggs, and yolks. Add the vanilla; mix well. Cool to room temperature.
2. In a separate bowl, beat the butter until creamy. Beat the liquor into the butter.
3. Slowly add the butter mixture to the egg mixture, beating continuously. The egg mixture and the butter mixture must have a similar temperature or they will not combine. If you have trouble combining them, refrigerate until they are the same temperature. Beat until blended.
4. Divide the frosting in two halves. Flavor one half with the cocoa, mixing it well. Flavor other half with the lemon juice, mixing it well.

Zucchini Bread

Makes one 8-inch loaf

3 medium-size zucchini
Unsalted butter, for pans
Bread crumbs, for pans
3 eggs
1 cup vegetable oil
1 1/2 cups sugar
2 teaspoons pure vanilla extract
2 cups sifted all-purpose flour
1/4 teaspoon baking powder
2 teaspoons baking soda
3 teaspoons ground cinnamon
1/2 teaspoon salt
1 cup raisins
1 cup chopped walnuts

1. Peel and grate the zucchini. Place them in a sieve and let them drain for 30 minutes.
2. Preheat the oven to 375°. Grease one 8-by-5-by-3-inch loaf pan or cake pan of your choice. Dust the pan with bread crumbs.
3. Beat the eggs lightly in a large bowl. Stir in the oil, sugar, grated zucchini, and vanilla.
4. Sift the flour, baking powder, baking soda, cinnamon, and salt together and stir into the egg mixture. Add the raisins and nuts; combine.
5. Spoon the batter into the prepared pan. Bake for 60 minutes.
6. Cool for 10 minutes in the pan, then remove and let cool completely before cutting.

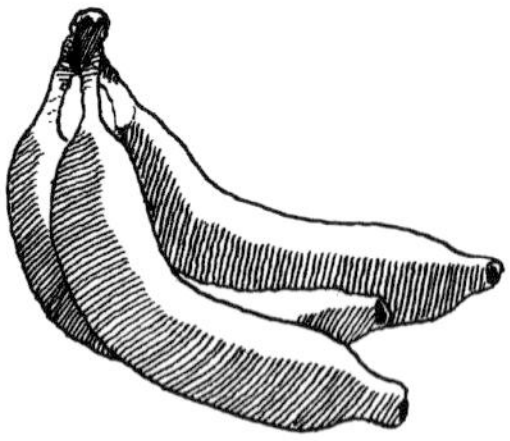

A

B

C

Index to Recipes